Contents

To Mark Willis
and
New York City

They sustain me.

Introduction

Form Follows Finance is not the title I preferred for this book initially, as the phrase represents only part of my argument, and, like Louis Sullivan's famous and frequently misconstrued axiom "form follows function," it can easily be mistaken as narrowly deterministic. Rather, I liked *Vernaculars of Capitalism*, a title that better reflects two issues that must be held in tandem to understand how skyscrapers and skylines took shape through the first half of the twentieth century. Of primary importance were the economic and programmatic formulas for quality office space: these tended to standardize highrise design everywhere. Modifying this template were local conditions: the historic grid of blocks and lots, municipal codes, and zoning caused tall buildings to develop distinctive forms, and thus created a vernacular unique to each city. The term vernacular usually applies to structures of relatively small scale, often domestic, which are less *designed* than *evolved* in response to functional demands and to the particulars of place. In contrast to histories of the skyscraper that focus on famous architects, corporate headquarters, or the "schools" of Chicago and New York, this study treats tall office buildings as vernacular architecture. It views highrise designs typologically, identifying different characteristic forms in the two cities, and interprets these as the product of standard market formulas and specific urban situations.

Skyscraper history is commonly divided—principally on stylistic grounds—into two major periods that break at mid-century. The earlier phase, which began with the first tall office buildings in the last quarter of the nineteenth century and continued into the Great Depression, subsumed several styles, including historicist designs, the "proto-modernism" of the Chicago School, and Art Deco of the 1920s. A second period reached full force after the long hiatus in construction during the Depression and World War II. There are many valid reasons for seeing a major change in highrise design and construction at this time, especially the introduction of new building materials and engineering technologies, but the primary basis for viewing the 1950s as a watershed has centered on the hegemonic influence of high modernism.[1]

The periodization proposed by this study likewise divides at the 1940s and 1950s, but is based on different factors. I call the earlier phase the *vernacular period* in order to emphasize how in these years building forms were of necessity connected to the environment; *light* and *site* are key words for the vernacular period. Before the 1940s, office interiors depended principally on sunlight for illumination, and buildings thus related to the boundaries of their lots in ways that became unnecessary after the introduction of fluorescent lighting and air conditioning. I use *international* to describe the period after 1950. Although evocative of the International Style aesthetics of steel, glass, spatial volumes, and structural expression, the term is not intended to be exclusively stylistic: rather, it suggests the relationship—or lack thereof—between the form of a building and its site and surroundings. In this framework, international refers to the fact that advances in technology as well as changes in architectural ideology made tall buildings independent of their sites and essentially interchangeable from one city to another. Even postmodern contextualism is international by this definition.

Form Follows Finance concentrates on the skyscrapers and commercial cores of New York and Chicago from the late nineteenth century to the 1940s. (*Skyscraper* is used here as a synonym for office buildings, but very tall structures can house hotels, apartments, hospitals, loft space, etc.; nevertheless, skyscrapers are most often erected for office use, since that type of space usually reaps the highest rents per square foot.) Today, the skylines of most American downtowns are dominated by a dozen or more towers, but as late as 1960, only three other cities contained more than two buildings taller than twenty-five stories: Detroit had eight, Philadelphia six, and Pittsburgh, five.[2] Thus, for the first half of the twentieth century, New York and Chicago constituted the country's only skyscraper metropolises.

The text is organized in two main parts: Part I focuses on the development of typical building forms in each city, while Part II addresses the urban scale and the economics of real estate speculation that shape skylines. The vernacular period is divided into its two significant phases. In the first section, the focus begins in the 1890s, that is, in the decade after the early elevator office buildings, the much-mooted "first skyscrapers," and spans the 1910s.[3] During this period, Chicago and New York offered strikingly different models of skyscraper design and urban development—one regulated, the other laissez-faire. Chicago's impressive first decade as the leader in highrise construction had stopped short in 1893 due to a real estate recession born of overbuilding in previous years. In response, the city council limited building height to 130 feet, the equivalent of ten or eleven stories, and although the cap moved up to 260 feet over the next three decades, the limitation discouraged development. As late as 1923, a survey showed only ninety-two buildings of ten to twenty-two stories in the Loop. In New York where height was unrestricted, after 1889, when metal-skeleton construction was allowed by the building code, towers proliferated. By 1913, Manhattan boasted nearly one thousand buildings of eleven to twenty stories, and fifty-one of between twenty-one and sixty stories. Thus, while New York had slightly more than double Chicago's population in 1920 (5.6 million versus 2.7 million residents), it had more than ten times the number of tall buildings.[4]

The second phase of the vernacular period spanned the 1920s through the early 1930s, years when the total volume of office space more than doubled in both cities. Zoning laws radically altered the skyscrapers and skylines of each metropolis. New York's ordinance dictated the characteristic setback forms of the period; Chicago's law offered a more limited

9

formula for towers. Other scholars have discussed the similarities in both cities' twenties setbacks; here, the differences are emphasized. During the boom of the 1920s, New York, with its more active speculative environment, pulled farther ahead of Chicago in the number and height of its towers. The tallest building in the Loop in 1931 was the forty-five-story, 612-foot Board of Trade; in Manhattan, sixteen spires exceeded that height, including the Empire State Building, at 1,250 feet.

An outline, rather than a building-by-building opus, this study presents a skeletal argument, filled out by many illustrations of buildings that are usually treated as types, rather than as individual architectural solutions. Rarely do I discuss single buildings at length, and I downplay the role of architects as designers to emphasize the parameters fixed by municipal regulations and by functional, structural, and programmatic demands. This is not to say that architects are merely technicians or decorators of predetermined forms; I discuss the example of Raymond Hood, a designer who was able to manipulate both clients and the zoning envelope to produce buildings that broke the conventional mold, while still satisfying the rules of cost and return. But exceptions are not the point of this work; the aim is to describe the broad principles that affect all skyscrapers and to explain how these universal factors, adapted to the historical land patterns and codes of a particular city, generated typical formal solutions, widely applied for similar sites.

Along these lines of analyzing the normative, Part II emphasizes speculative buildings—the majority of skyscrapers in every period—and examines how the economics of development and real estate cycles affect building heights and spatial distribution. The rise of the secularized skylines of American cities from the late nineteenth century have often been interpreted as representations of corporate power and advertising. This study argues that skyscrapers should best be understood both as the locus of busines and as businesses themselves.

In focusing on economics as a chief determinant of form and on the influence of functional requirements and municipal codes, my analysis departs from previous skyscraper histories. Other accounts have centered mainly on the roles of architects, engineers, and clients, on technological and structural innovations, and on issues of style. From the 1940s, polemical historians such as Sigfried Giedion and Carl Condit celebrated steel skeletons and glass skins and viewed the tall buildings of the "Chicago School" of the 1880s and 1890s as pioneers of the aesthetics of structure of the modern movement.[5] (It is ironic to note that despite their espousal of functionalism, these authors paid little attention to the relationship of internal function and outward form: there were no floor plans in any of Condit's volumes on Chicago skyscrapers and only one in Giedion's book.) Countering the "myth of the Chicago School," more recent authors have pointed out the bias of modernist historians and have underscored the central importance of ornament in the work of Sullivan and others. Historians Robert Bruegmann and Daniel Bluestone have discussed the decorative programs of facades and ornate lobbies of Loop office buildings and of their clients' aspirations in terms of cultural expression.[6] Others have pursued the perspective of cultural history for New York buildings of the late nineteenth century and, especially, for the 1920s.[7]

Like the rivalry between Chicago and New York for the world's tallest building, writers have often championed one metropolis or the other. A key dispute centers on which city should be considered the birthplace of the skyscraper, a debate that depends entirely on how one defines the building type. Partisans of Chicago have stressed technological innovation—the combination of the elevator and metal-skeleton construction in a multi-story office block, whereas advocates of New York have emphasized tallness—relative height compared to surrounding structures—as the salient feature. These characteristics continued to be seen as representative through the early twentieth century. In *The Skyscraper* (surprisingly, the only book-length survey on this building type), Paul Goldberger cited the "rigorous theory" and "structural honesty" as attributes of Chicago's "commercial style," which he contrasted with New York's "striving for height," historical eclecticism, and devotion to "pure visual pleasure."[8] Similarly, Leland Roth's summary typified the textbook treatment of the differences between the cities: "While Chicago architects had focused on frank expression of the frame through banks of broad windows, in New York the emphasis was on expressive height and on the adaptation of contemporary and historic modes to the tall building."[9]

As generalizations, such statements are not inaccurate, but from the perspective of this study, they neglect important issues. One is interiors, which were virtually indistinguishable in the two cities, either in plan or in design. Like most writings on skyscrapers, these discussions are concerned principally with the composition of facades, and hardly at all with the three-dimensional form—except for height, which is considered only with respect to expressive motives. Buildings in New York may have been "striving for height," but the number of stories erected was also driven by economic formulas and market rents. In Chicago from 1893 to 1923, heights were restricted to between ten and twenty-two stories by municipal codes. In the twenties, Manhattan towers often stretched twice as high as those in the Loop, because Chicago's zoning law limited maximum volume, while New York's left a portion of the site unrestricted.

For skyscrapers of the 1920s, writing has generally continued to focus on one city or the other, and there have been few attempts at comparative analysis.[10] My own efforts were prompted by a commission from The Art Institute of Chicago for an essay in the catalog *Chicago Architecture and Design, 1923–1993*.[11] For that stimulating assignment, I am grateful to John Zukowsky, whose expertise on his city is matched by his creativity in placing it in a broader context. Another of his ideas was the 1984 exhibit and catalog, *Chicago and New York: Architectural Interactions*, one of the few attempts to explore the relationships between the two cities. An essay by Carol Hershelle Krinsky detailed inter-city connections of architects and clients and described parallel responses to certain urban building types and planning problems.[12] Although the article stressed similarities, it concluded by observing: "New York and Chicago do not look alike." Their different characters were simply described and attributed to a variety of factors, including geographic setting and historic platting. My aim is to explain how these and other conditions operated to produce the two cities' distinct vernaculars.

To this end, several books have inspired my thinking, though in ways not clearly related to the topics outlined heree. Jane Jacobs's *Death and Life of Great American Cities* and *Delirious New York*, by Dutch architect Rem Koolhaas, bowled me over when I first read them in the early and late 1970s, respectively.[13] Utterly antithetical (except for their mutual passion for New York's diversity), both books stated ideas about the city that for me had emotional resonance. I immediately identified with Jacobs's description of successful streets and was deeply impressed by both the simplicity of her method—looking hard at cities and thinking about how they work—and by the clarity of her prose. Her analysis satisfies the test of common sense; I hope my argument meets that same standard. The antipode of Jacob's empiricism is *Delirious New York*, which, as the title suggests, has little truck with reason. Koolhaas celebrates the irrational, or as he would have it, the suprarational character of "Manhattanism" and the "culture of congestion." Although presented as a history, his text is not concerned with veracity; yet, anyone who has marveled at the almost absurd density of the skyscraper island will recognize something that seems true to spirit in his portrait.

Two other influences are historians. One is the late Warren Susman, whose essays on American mass culture and social change—particularly in the 1920s and 1930s—are for me models of scholarship in the way they survey a broad spectrum of popular culture and at the same time explicate the power of ideas in shaping societal values.[14] His synthesis is offered without the undertone of ideological critique that often surfaces in cultural history. A similar marshalling of the mundane world to explain larger urban systems is accomplished by William Cronon in *Nature's Metropolis*, in which he explains nineteenth-century Chicago's rise to dominance by connecting the growth of the city to the restructuring, by economics, of the vast hinterland. In Cronon's thesis, the "natural advantages" of geography are less important to the city's development than the "second nature" of human interventions, in particular the railroad; as forests became lumber and plains yielded grain, railroads first centered this supply of commodities, then exported the goods.[15] At a less majestic scale, by emphasizing the economic determinants on building forms and urban development, my efforts to relate the space of the single office to the silhouette of the city owe some inspiration to Cronon.

This book is not traditional architectural history. It ignores the litany of famous figures and events connected with the skyscraper, and rarely names the architects of building merely cited (that is, I prefer not to privilege the architects' role over that of others of the team).[16] Since the text groups buildings in phases, the specific dates are not particularly important, except as they relate to real estate cycles. (Dates given refer to the year of completion, but the reader is warned that sources for these are often inexact.) Because it offers an approach quite different from such standard themes as style, "schools," structure, or cultural expression, this study may be seen as revisionist. However, many of the arguments simply retrieve points made in the period's professional literature by architects, general contractors, building owners and managers, and writers in industry publications; a variety of these sources are quoted at length in the text.

In his 1896 essay "The Tall Office Building Artistically Considered," Louis Sullivan advised that the universal law "form ever follows function" should be applied to highrise structures. He was not referring to three-dimensional form, but to the symbolic expression of different interior use on the facade; indeed, he declined to discuss issues such as floor plans, light courts, or mechanical systems, because they were concerned "strictly with the economics of the building," and therefore had no aesthetic value. In emotive prose Sullivan enjoined the tall office building to be "lofty":

> It must be every inch a proud and soaring thing, rising in sheer exaltation from bottom to top...without a single dissenting line...it is the new, the unexpected, the eloquent peroration of most bald, most sinister, most forbidding conditions.[17]

Sullivan scorned the social and economic forces that fostered the modern office building.[18] Indeed, through the early twentieth century, disdain for the skyscraper was common among conservative architects and critics who believed that the commercial nature of the tall office building was incompatible with the art of architecture.

Quite a different view and tone was advanced by George Hill, an expert on commercial real estate and frequent contributor to *Architectural Record*. Apparently irked by other articles in the journal emphasizing the art of the skyscraper, he protested:

> The writer wishes to state once and for all, and as strongly as it can be put, that the only measure of a success of an office building is the average net return from rentals for a period of, say, fifteen years. Everything put into the building that is unnecessary, every cubic foot that is used for purely ornamental purposes beyond that needed to express its use and to make it harmonize with others of its class, is a waste—is, to put it in plain English, perverting some one's money.[19]

Between these poles of exaltation and economy, there was considerable middle ground. One of the most acute writers on skyscrapers from around the turn of the century was Barr Ferree, an editor of *Engineering Magazine*. In an address to the annual convention of the American Institute of Architects in 1893, he observed:

> Current American architecture is not a matter of art, but of business. A building must pay or there will be no investor ready with the money to meet its cost. This is at once the curse and the glory of American architecture.[20]

I share Ferree's view that the commercial nature of the skyscraper, while a defining force, is no impediment to beauty. Indeed, structures such as the Empire State Building or Board of Trade are magnificent not because they were designed by great architects, but because their designers worked intelligently within a formula with its own beautiful economy.

"Form follows finance" is axiomatic, but it is not, like Sullivan's idea of functionalism, a natural law. Alone, it is not adequate to explain why tall buildings took different forms in different cities. Other factors—the effects of human actions and decisions and of imposed patterns and policies—

affect design solutions. As this study illustrates, the formulas of finance responded to the particular urban conditions of New York and Chicago to produce distinct *vernaculars of capitalism.*

Why, then, does my title declare so unambiguously that *Form Follows Finance?* Because my friends and colleagues argued that "vernacular" sounded dull, while the alliterative phrase was snappy, like an advertising slogan. I resisted their pressure at first, since I had used the title for an earlier essay. But sitting around Rosalie's dinner table last spring, my friends insisted I would be crazy not to use it again, and as Kevin encouraged: "Frankly, it will sell more books." This compelling rationale—so analogous to my analysis of the commercial values of skyscrapers—seemed good enough reason to comply.

Thanks are due to a great many friends and colleagues who helped me along the way. This book assembles pieces presented in several earlier papers and essays, and it is important to recognize those who drew me into their plans and spurred me on with deadlines. I was pleased to participate in a two-part conference on early-twentieth-century New York sponsored by the Social Science Research Council; David Ward and Olivier Zunz were the editors of the resulting volume, *The Landscape of Modernity*, in which I first used the title "Form Follows Finance" for my article on the Empire State Building. As noted, the assignment from John Zukowsky and The Art Institute of Chicago was a boon, for it forced me to look closely at Chicago skyscrapers and opened up a new way of thinking about how building forms are affected by particular cities. Carol Clark invited me to speak on the history of New York's 1916 zoning law at a conference sponsored by the city's Department of City Planning. Naomi Miller and Roberta Moudry chaired stimulating sessions on the American city at the annual conventions of the Society of Architectural Historians in 1993 and 1994, at which I outlined the two parts of this book. For all of these opportunities and interactions, I am grateful.

During the research for these various projects, a number of people at institutions and archives were exceptionally helpful. At my home base, Columbia's Avery Architectural and Fine Arts Library, Angela Giral, Avery Librarian, and Janet Parks, Curator of Drawings, have always responded generously to my requests. At the Ryerson and Burnham Libraries of The Art Institute of Chicago, Mary Woolever has been cheerfully supportive. I benefited from a research grant from the Hagley Museum and Library to spend time in their archives, and I am grateful to the staff for their assistance and to the museum's director, Glenn Porter, for his interest in my work. A number of scholars have shared their expertise or files with me; in particular, I want to thank Sally Kitt Chappell, Robert Breugmann, and Gail Fenske. John Margolies introduced me to postcard collecting; the evidence of this obsession is apparent throughout this book. Penny Kleinman kindly shared her excellent collection of Chicago cards with me.

I have been helped enormously by good friends who have served as sounding boards, readers, boosters, and, occasionally, skeptics. I am especially grateful to Hilary Ballon, Barry Bergdoll, Mary Beth Betts, Andrew Dolkart, Alex Garvan, Rosalie Genevro, Kenneth Jackson, Kevin Lippert, Marc Weiss, and Mark Willis for their contributions to and enthusiasm for this project. I am particularly indebted to Marc Weiss, who shared his expertise in the rich, but essentially unstudied field of real estate history, directing me to the essential texts and feeding me ideas. In more general ways, other longtime friends on whom I test my thinking, Rosemarie Bletter, Michelle Bogart, Richard Cleary, Dennis Doordan, Deborah Gardner, and Joel Saunders, deserve thanks.

The Graham Foundation for Advanced Studies in the Fine Arts provided generous support for this publication. At an earlier stage of my research, I was assisted by a grant from University Seminars at Columbia.

Heartfelt thanks to Allison Saltzman, who designed and edited the book with keen intelligence, great patience, and sensibilites well matched with my own. To Kevin Lippert and the entire operation of Princeton Architectural Press, my complete admiration for what they do.

Sky Line, New York City.

Fig. 1 New York's skyline, c.1913, features multiple towers.
Fig. 2 Chicago, Michigan Avenue, c.1913, where heights are capped.

Part I

Vernaculars of Capitalism

Overview

Fundamental factors of function and economics make tall buildings every-where take similar forms, yet skyscrapers in New York and Chicago devel-oped very differently in the first half of this century. Some have explained these variations as expressions of different design personalities or philoso-phies—the Chicago and New York "schools." This study argues that the variations can best be understood as products of standard real estate for-mulas that were modified by local conditions such as the city's historic grid, municipal regulations, and zoning. Distinct vernaculars of capitalism evolved in each city from this combination of economic logic and the par-ticulars of place.

"A machine that makes the land pay" was the apt definition of a sky-scraper offered by Cass Gilbert in 1900, a decade before he designed the Woolworth Building.[1] As George Hill, an authority on commercial real estate, explained in *The Architectural Record*: "An office building's prime and only object is to earn the greatest possible return for its owners, which means that it must present the maximum of rentable space possible on the lot, with every portion of it fully lit."[2] This insistence on the linkage between profit and program is fundamental to commercial architecture,

Fig. 3 View north on Broadway, New York, c.1915. Note narrow facades and tall towers.
Left to right: Trinity, U.S. Realty, Singer, City Investing Company, and Woolworth Buildings.

Fig. 4 View north on South LaSalle Street, Chicago, early 1920s. Towerless quarter-block buildings.
Left: Federal Reserve Bank, Illinois Continental and Commercial Bank.
Right: Illinois Merchants Bank, Rookery Building.

Fig. 5 Tall towers and pyramidal setbacks characterize Lower Manhattan's skyline in the 1930s.
Fig. 6 Chicago's Loop in the 1930s presents a flat-roofed plateau punctuated by a few
truncated towers.

where the function of a building is to produce rents, and economic considerations govern design decisions. This section first examines programmatic factors that determined the dimensions and layout of standard office units and floor plans, chiefly the need for well-lighted interiors. It then analyzes how those universal factors were adapted to individual sites and urban situations to produce typical formal solutions in New York and Chicago from the 1890s through the 1910s, and in the 1920s and 1930s.

During the first period, the characteristic skyscraper form in New York was the tower, often tall and slender, with a floor plan arranged around a compact core of circulation and mechanical services. A tower was the most profitable way to build in a city where lots were generally small and height was not regulated. In contrast, in Chicago where heights were capped and lots were generally large, the dominant type was a rectangular box penetrated at the center or rear by a large light court. Thus the early twentieth-century silhouette of Manhattan bristled with towers, while the skyline of Chicago was relatively low, flat-topped, and homogeneous. *(Figs. 1–4)*

In the 1920s, building forms in both cities changed dramatically as a result of new zoning ordinances. New York's 1916 law encouraged the "wedding cake" setbacks, often topped with a thin central tower. In Chicago, the 1923 zoning law permitted a tower to rise above the old height limit, but restricted its total volume. Two new formal types evolved from this regulation: a composite big base and tiny tower; and an integrated base-and-tower scheme. As buildings took characteristic forms from the local laws and land use, so did skylines. In distant views, Manhattan often looked like mountains and pinnacles, whereas Chicago seen from above seemed more like a plateau with a few isolated, truncated towers. *(Figs. 5, 6)*

Since the 1950s, these distinctive vernaculars have been voided by advances in technology, zoning reforms, the orthodoxy of high modernism, and, more recently, the stylistics of postmodernism. As the postscript at the end of Part I suggests, in the international phase, the differences in skyscraper design and urbanism in New York, Chicago, and everywhere diminished in response to the forces of finance, market values of design, and prevailing theories of urbanism.

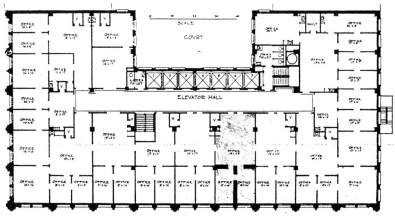

Fig. 7 Plan of typical upper floor, Monroe Building, Chicago (1912). Note "T" layout of offices.

Real Estate Rules for Skyscraper Design

Skyscrapers were and still are designed from the inside out: from the smallest cell, to the full-floor plan, to the three-dimensional form. The first step was to determine the dimensions of the smallest unit—the single office—which was a room with one or two windows. *(Figs. 7, 8)* This module was then reproduced as many times as possible within an efficient floor plan. Even when space was not partitioned into offices, but pooled in large areas, the "phantom" office governed the full-floor plan, which was then multiplied by the desired number of stories. Until zoning laws were passed that dictated a setback massing, most skyscrapers simply reproduced the same plan floor above floor.

Natural light was the most important factor in setting the dimensions of the office, because until the introduction of fluorescent bulbs in the 1940s, sunlight was the principal source of illumination for interiors. Although electric wiring was universal by the 1890s, incandescent bulbs remained weak and inefficient. The main form of artificial light, desk-top lamps, produced about three to four foot-candles (one foot-candle is the amount of light on a surface held one foot away from a burning candle). Outdoors, summer sunlight radiates about 10,000 foot-candles, and even cloudy days can provide

Fig. 8 Individual office, Peoples Gas Company Building, Chicago (1911).

200 to 500 foot-candles. Inside, daylight levels average about fifty to one hundred foot-candles, although ten is typical for a room with good exposure.[3] *(Fig. 9)* The standard for adequate lighting changed over the years: one survey in New York in 1916 recommended eight to nine foot-candles; in the 1920s it rose to ten to twelve foot-candles; in the 1930s, spurred by aggressive sales tactics of large power companies, some experts urged twenty-five foot-candles.[4] Indirect lighting from large ceiling lamps was considered the most healthful type of illumination since it produced the fewest and faintest shadows, but using multiple lightbulbs added considerable heat to a room—one 500-watt bulb gave off the equivalent of one pound of steam per hour—which posed problems in hot weather.[5]

The quality and rentability of office space thus depended on large windows and high ceilings that allowed daylight to penetrate as deeply as possible into the interior. Ceiling heights were at least ten to twelve feet, and single windows were as big as possible without being too heavy to open—generally about four to five feet wide and six to eight feet high. The "Chicago window," a large, fixed central pane with operable side sashes, was another solution. Paired or grouped in multiples, windows gave rhythm to the facade. The main reason for the spacing that did not

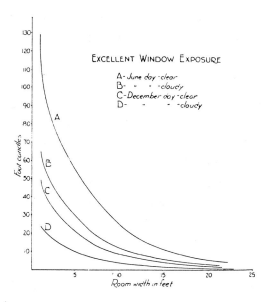

Fig. 9 Measurements of daylight illumination in office buildings,
showing decrease in amount of light, according to distance from windows.

correspond directly to the structural bay, though, was to allow for the easy partitioning of the interior into small, individual offices. Many buildings had mechanical ventilating and cooling systems (there was no air conditioning until the 1930s), but open windows provided the fresh air vital to comfort, especially in summer months.

The need for natural light also affected the depth of offices, which was the distance from the windows to the innermost wall or public corridor. The maximum of twenty to twenty-eight feet was almost universally observed, and changed only slightly until the introduction of fluorescent lighting. What the industry called "economical depth" referred to the fact that shallow, better-lit space produced higher revenues than deep and therefore dark interiors. Or as George Hill asserted: "After a certain point is reached, no more money can be obtained...no matter what its depth."[6] For example, a 1923 survey of values in Boston showed that offices fifteen feet deep leased for $3.00 per square foot, while space twenty-five feet brought only $2.60, and fifty feet, only

$1.65.[7] Since the latter cost nearly as much to build and operate, but netted only about half the income, the logic of producing first-quality space was clear. Architect Harvey Wiley Corbett stated the general point simply: "It is better business to construct less building, and have shallow offices well lighted, than to have more building with deep spaces poorly lighted. In other words, it is better to have less space—less capital investment—permanently rented at a high figure than too much space partially rented at a low figure."[8]

The early 1890s was still a period of experimentation with efficiency of floor plans, but by the early 1900s, with experience and with the increasing professionalization of building owners and managers, the layout became quite standard.[9] In single-room offices, furniture was used to define the different work areas, or, if large enough, the depth from window to public corridor could be partitioned, generally with translucent glass to gain borrowed light. *(Fig. 10)* For larger suites, one entered from the hall into a room that served as reception and staff areas. Beyond were the private offices, generally eight to ten feet wide (so that two fit within a standard structural bay), and about twelve to fourteen feet deep.[10] The so-called "T" arrangement allowed two private rooms, each with a window, and a reception area large enough for a stenographer, files, and a waiting room. This layout can be seen in nearly every floor plan in this book.

Power and rank (and, as a result, gender) were reflected in the spatial arrangement. Executives claimed corner offices, or at least an exterior windowed room, while secretaries and other staff were relegated to the deeper, darker spaces. The hierarchy was described in the 1950s by Earle Shultz and Walter Simmons in *Offices in the Sky*:

> Of course the boss had to have his private office next to the window with the light coming in over his shoulder. In some cases his secretary worked in the office, too, but usually she and other clerical help used the reception room space between the private office and the corridor wall. To get maximum light into the reception room, the partition dividing it from the private office was glass. Sometimes this glass was opaqued to prevent people waiting in the reception room from seeing into the private office.[11]

Fig. 10 Pair of typical offices, New York, 1920s.

An advertisement for the Straus Building in Chicago shows such an arrangement. *(Fig. 11)*

Businesses that employed many clerks or secretaries required large open floors for their operations. Unpartitioned spaces afforded better light, housed workers more efficiently, and also allowed for eagle-eyed supervision, as the photograph of "The Metropolitan Belles" illustrates. *(Figs. 12, 13)* Major companies that needed to centralize files and coordinate many departments found it desirable to build a headquarters that served their requirements and, unlike leased space, ensured control over the term of their occupancy. A corporate headquarters, of course, could also project status and serve as a kind of advertising.

Nevertheless, throughout the first decades of the century, most buildings were speculative, and over eighty percent of tenants leased suites of less than 1,000 square feet, which was the equivalent of four or

This Suite at $130 a Month
in Chicago's Finest Office Building

Fig. 11 Advertisement for office space, Straus Building, Chicago, 1923.

five office units.[12] Indeed, the most profitable strategy for a building owner was to rent a large number of small offices, since such leases paid a higher rate per square foot. Having a majority of small tenants offered other advantages: the tenants did not move in a body, leaving the building with high vacancies, nor did they overload the elevator service at time-clock hours.

This analysis was one of eight points of economic design set forth by Chicago developer Owen F. Aldis while collaborating with the architects Holabird and Roche on the Marquette Building (1891–94), which was considered a model of efficient planning. *(Fig. 66)* Aldis, who began his career as the financial agent and building manager for the Boston investors Peter and Shepherd Brooks, then formed his own company, and was by the turn of the century responsible for nearly one-fifth of all the office space in the Loop. His "eight fundamentals" of profitable development emphasized good light and

Fig. 12 Workers in Metropolitan Life Insurance Company Building, New York, 1896.
Note lamps at each station.

air, attractive lobbies and corridors, easy circulation, and good building service
and maintenance. Most important, he advocated creating only high-quality
interiors: "Second-class space costs as much to build as first-class space.
Therefore build no second-class space." Aldis's definition of "first-class" space
was a maximum depth of twenty-four feet from window to wall.[13]

Facades also became part of an owner's marketing strategy, for as Barr

Ferree noted in *The Modern Office Building* in 1896:

> The exterior of a building is generally the criterion by which its success is
> measured....But office buildings have so little to offer within in the way of
> ornament or of art, that the general public, and perhaps the architectural
> public, have fallen into the habit of judging them by their facades...a fine-

Fig. 13 Interior, Peoples Gas Company Building, Chicago (1911).

ly designed office building has now a greater commercial value than one that is badly designed...and so the facade has a monetary value in these buildings which it does not always have in other structures.[14]

Real estate rules also affected massing and height, although the three-dimensional development of a building depended on the individual site and city, in particular, on the typical size of blocks and lots, and on munici-

pal codes that regulated height, bulk, or lot coverage. Thus, while office plans and interiors were virtually identical in all cities, changing little from the turn of the century through the twenties, skyscrapers in New York and Chicago presented very different formal types when viewed from the outside. The following sections analyze how the universals of program and profit combined with historical patterns and local conditions to produce the two cities' distinct vernaculars of capitalism.

WORLD BLDG.　　　　AM. TRACT　PARK ROW BUILDING　　　WESTERN UNION　　　LIBERTY BUILDING
POST OFFICE　　　SOCIETY BLDG.　　ST. PAUL BLDG.　　TELEGRAPH BLDG.　　　　　　　　　　　WASHINGTON
　　　FIDELITY

Fig. 14 Panoramic view of New York skyline, c.1900.

New York to 1916

New York, "the capital of capitalism," represented the laissez-faire model of
skyscraper development. For whatever reasons—the vitality of its commercial environment, the urge to advertise, or the waterbound confines of
Lower Manhattan—the pressures to multiply the value of land by stacking
story upon story were enormous. The city imposed no restrictions on the
height or lot coverage of structures other than tenements before the passage of its first zoning law in 1916. In theory, a property owner could build
straight up from the lot lines as far into the heavens as he or she desired, or
as money allowed. After code approval of steel-cage construction in 1889,
office buildings regularly began to top sixteen and more stories. A turn-of-
the-century postcard view of the skyline seen from the Hudson River
showed nearly a dozen office towers eclipsing the landmark of the nineteenth century, the spire of Trinity Church. *(Fig. 14)* These included the

Manhattan Life Insurance, American Surety, and Empire Buildings along Broadway, and nearer to City Hall, the St. Paul, Park Row, American Tract Society, and World Buildings. All exceeded 300 feet and thus surpassed Chicago's tallest skyscraper, the Masonic Temple. At 386 feet, the Park Row Building, completed in 1898, was the world's tallest office structure.[15] By 1913, the Woolworth Building stretched twice as high, to 792 feet.

"The state of things in New York is largely brought about by its rapidly developing and changing character," observed William Birkmire, author of an important early study of the skyscraper of 1900. "The island is so narrow and its trade centre so near one end, that the tendency of each trade is not only to flock to one spot, but to crowd as near the centre as possible, thus making the price of land down-town simply tremendous."[16] Accordingly, the value of proximity in business produced a spiral of increased land costs, premium rents, and taller buildings.

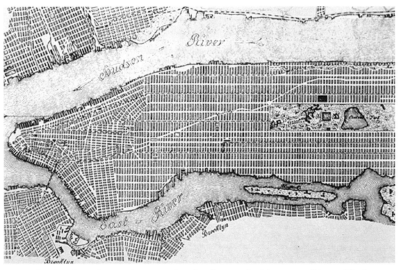

Fig. 15 Map of Manhattan, showing colonial and post-colonial pattern of Lower Manhattan and 1811 Commissioners' Plan.

In New York, three major factors combined to produce the city's first characteristic skyscraper form, the tower: high demand for commercial space, lack of regulation of building height, and the historic mapping of Manhattan with its first colonial pattern of streets and blocks, post-colonial skewed grids, and rectangular blocks of the 1811 Commissioners' Plan. *(Fig. 15)*

The city's many relatively small lots created an economic logic for towers. In the financial district of Lower Manhattan, the area of the original colonial settlement, land was first sold as lots rather than as frontage, and ownership was broken up into many parcels that for well over a hundred years were occupied by profitable lowrise buildings. Large sites were thus difficult and expensive to assemble, and, unlike Chicago in 1871, no great fire conveniently cleared the way for redevelopment just at the period of rapid corporate expansion.

Farther uptown in the regular grid of avenues and cross streets of the 1811 Commissioners' Plan, the standard blocks measured 200 feet wide (north-south) and about 600 to 800 feet long (east-west). Lots were generally 100 feet deep (half the width of the block) and tended to be divided

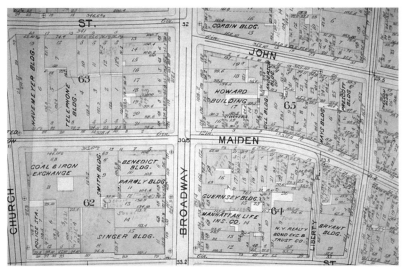

Fig. 16 Bromley's *Atlas of the City of New York, Borough of Manhattan*, 1899.
Detail of Broadway and Maiden Lane.

into 25-foot frontages or multiples thereof, which were suitable dimensions for individual homes or shops.[17] Thus, despite the regularity of the blocks, parcels within them tended to be small. *(Fig. 16)* Although the most active period of skyscraper development uptown came after 1920, from 1900 to 1910, several very conspicuous structures pioneered north of City Hall, in particular the Flatiron Building, the Times Building, and the campanile of Metropolitan Life. *(Figs. 37, 22, 152)*

In prestige areas like Wall Street, very tall buildings often rose on small or constricted sites. *(Figs. 17–24)* An extreme case was an eighteen-story office tower erected on a lot at the southeast corner of Broadway and Wall Street that measured only 30 x 40 feet. The Gillender Building (1897) on the northwest corner of Wall and Broad Streets rose eighteen stories on a corner site only 25 x 73 feet.[18] The Commercial Cable Building (1897) piled twenty-one stories on a 45 x 155-foot lot adjacent to the New York Stock Exchange. The nearly twin, twenty-three-story Trinity and U.S. Realty Buildings (1905, 1906) occupied sites of approximately 67 x 267 and 61 x 275 feet, while the Empire Building (1898) rose nearby on a lot 78 x 223 feet.

Figs. 17–20 New York towers.
Top: Gillender Building (1897), St. Paul Building (1899).
Bottom: Park Row Building (1898), Bankers Trust Building (1912).

Liberty Tower,
New York

Adams Express
Company Building,
New York City.

Figs. 21–24 New York towers.
Top: Trinity Building (1905), Times Building (1903).
Bottom: Liberty Tower (1910), Adams Express Company Building (1914).

Figs. 25, 26 Commercial Cable Building, New York (1897). View and plan.

Some might consider a building of such proportions a slab rather than a tower; however, the term is used simply to refer to the building's extreme verticality.

Towers proliferated on such sites because they were efficient and profitable. Offices could be arranged in a shallow ring of rentable space surrounding a central core of circulation and mechanical services. This plan maximized the area with good light and views, while minimizing costs, especially for expensive exterior walls. The compact core can be seen in the plans of the Commercial Cable, Trinity, and U.S. Realty Buildings. *(Figs. 26, 28, 29)* It was best suited for sites of around sixty to seventy feet wide, i.e., the sum of two twenty- to twenty-five-foot deep suites, plus an area for circulation and services. The appeal of this plan can be seen in a number of tall towers erected on squarish sites from the mid-1890s to the 1910s. The American Surety Building (1896) rose twenty-one stories on a lot 85 x 85 feet; the twenty-six-story St. Paul Building (1898) occupied an irregular lot of approximately 50 x 100 feet. The thirty-three-story Liberty

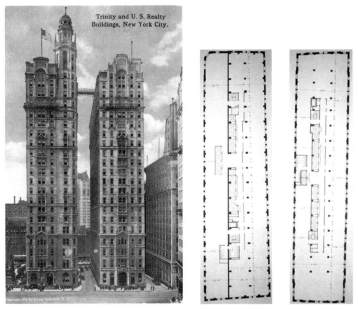

Figs. 27–29 Trinity and U.S. Realty Buildings, New York (1905, 1906). View and typical plans.

Tower (1910) occupied a corner lot of 58 x 82 feet at Liberty and Nassau Streets. An advertising brochure for the building promoted its "perfect light and ventilation and expressive tower plan of construction."[19] In 1910, the Gillender Building was demolished to erect the 540-foot, thirty-nine-story tower for Bankers Trust (1912) on a parcel about 75 feet square. *(Figs. 30–33)*

The assembly of several small lots into larger parcels became more frequent in the early 1900s. Larger lots could also profit from the compact-core plan since the additional elevators required by taller buildings could occupy the deep, and otherwise unrentable centers. However, good elevator service, which had been a challenge in the tallest buildings in the 1890s and early 1900s, only achieved sophisticated arrangement in central banks in the 1910s.

Buildings grew steadily taller for several reasons. A prerequisite was the demand for office space fueled by the city's burgeoning business sector.

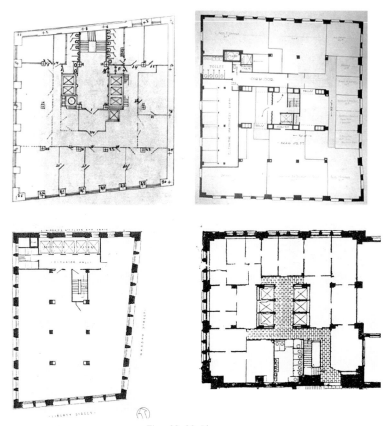

Figs. 30–33 Plans.
Top: American Surety Building (1896), Bankers Trust Company Building (1912).
Bottom: Liberty Tower (1910), Metropolitan Life Insurance Tower (1909).

Advances in engineering and construction made it possible to erect safer
and more efficient steel-frame structures and mechanical systems. Ego and
advertising also played a role, especially in the constructions of highly competitive individuals such as Frank W. Woolworth, or companies like
Metropolitan Life. However, the idea that skyscrapers advertised corporate
identity has been overstated by some scholars. Structures with prominence
on the skyline or with an advantageous site, such as fronting a park
(Woolworth Building) or on a triangle of streets (Flatiron or Times
Buildings), signaled the power of their corporate owners or their own

Fig. 34 Singer, City Investing, and Hudson Terminal Buildings, New York (all 1908).

status as a prime address. But at least as important an asset as good exposure on the skyline was protection of the exposure *inside*. Towers stretched high both for publicity and to capture direct sunlight.

That prestige and advertising affected decisions about height is apparent from the example of the 1909 tower for Metropolitan Life Insurance at Madison Square Park, where neither demand nor exorbitant land prices were factors driving up the number of stories. *(See Fig. 152, Part II)* Since 1893 when it moved uptown, the company had been expanding incrementally, and by 1907 it controlled the entire block between Twenty-third and Twenty-fourth Streets from Madison to Fourth Avenue.[20] The energy pushing the tower to 700 feet was clearly the competition to take the title of "world's tallest" from the 612-foot Singer Building. The soaring campanile was also intended to proclaim the success and stability of the company that had recently become the world's largest insurer. As a publicity booklet announced: "High and lofty, like a great sentinel keeping watch over the millions of policy holders and marking the fast-fleeting minutes of life, stands the Tower..."[21] From a business perspective, though, a fifty-story tower on a lot 75 x 85 feet was not the cheapest way to house the

Fig. 35 Equitable Building, New York (1915).

growing numbers of clerks and staff, and from the outset, about forty percent of the office space was set aside for rental.

The issue of extreme height and the three corporate spires—Singer,
Metropolitan Life, and Woolworth—that successively held the record in
the early 1900s is discussed in Part II. Each was in some way anomalous
with the standard rules of skyscraper development. More characteristic of
the majority of structures and of the real estate market's influence on form
were the City Investing Company (1908), Hudson Terminal (1908) *(both,
Fig. 34)*, Adams Express (1914) *(Fig. 24)*, and Equitable Buildings (1915).
(Fig. 35) These big, boxy containers seemed to be virtually extruded above
their lot lines for thirty stories or more. Unremarkable in their exteriors,

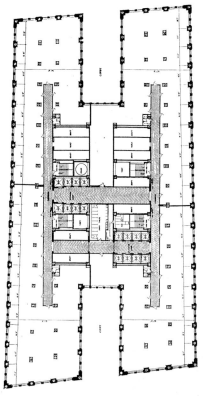

Fig. 36 Equitable Building plan, seventh through tenth floors.
Each floor was divided into approximately sixty-two office units.

they were, nevertheless, very efficient rental properties. The Equitable was not a corporate headquarters, but a savvy speculative project, a model of modernity calculated to return five percent on the owner's investment (as opposed, for example, to the Woolworth Building, which was widely known in real estate circles as a poor performer, earning only about two and a half to three percent). On completion in 1915, the 542-foot structure was the fifth tallest in New York, but with its 1.2 million square feet of rentable space, it was also the world's largest office building.[22]

An important aspect of "form follows finance" is the principle of *economic height*, aptly demonstrated by the design of the Equitable Building. *(Fig. 35)* Unlike *engineering height*, which was the number of stories that were structurally feasible, the economic height for a building referred to the number of stories that would produce the highest rate on the money invested. At some point in the construction of every skyscraper, the law of diminishing returns sets in, and rents for the additional stories do not cover costs. Taller buildings need extra foundations, bracing, and mechanical systems, but by far, the greatest price of height lies in the requirements of efficient vertical circulation. While elevators are expensive to build and operate (especially with attendants), their major cost accrues in the large amounts of space consumed by shafts.[23]

At the Equitable, the elevators determined the building's height. A main feature of the marketing was elevator service, which the management planned to promote as the the best in the world. Before any of the particulars of the design were set, a consultant, Charles E. Knox, was asked to calculate the number of cabs required to provide first-class service for a daily population of 50,000, and a rush-hour capacity per car of 300 persons every fifteen minutes. This was no small point; a reputation for slow service could impair rentability, as had happened with the Singer and Woolworth Buildings. Knox computed that with forty-eight elevators he could offer superior service for a thirty-six-story building, but not for the forty-two stories the client had hoped to build (although contemporary articles stated the building had thirty-six floors, as constructed, it has forty).[24]

Many factors influenced the Equitable Building's massing and height, including the size of the site, the cost of land, the amount of office space the owner believed could be rented, and the funds that could be mustered for the project. The large lot (approximately 167 x 310 feet) could have been developed with a soaring tower like that of the Woolworth (its site was only about 151 x 192), but instead was kept low and blocky, which was a less expensive type of construction. Since no office space was to be more than twenty-five to twenty-seven feet from a window, light courts had to be cut into the mass. The architects chose an H-plan, which put light wells on the main and rear facades, but afforded a long, straight line of offices on the sides. *(Fig. 36)* This was not a common arrangement in New York, nor was it well received in the press, which viewed the building as greedily oversized.

Figs. 37, 38 Flatiron Building, New York (1903), Conway Building, Chicago (1915).

The massing of the Equitable is instructive because it was designed by the Chicago firm of Graham, Anderson, Probst and White, the successors of Daniel H. Burnham and Co. It was a solution that could not have been constructed in their own city due to the limitations on height. The Equitable was fifty percent taller than any contemporary Chicago building, and this height rendered impracticable the use of a central light court that characterized large Loop buildings.[25]

It is instructive to compare the nearly identical facade treatment of the Equitable and Flatiron Buildings, both in New York, and the Conway Building in Chicago *(Figs. 37, 38)*, all produced by the same architectural office. Each structure was wrapped in virtually identical classical cladding. The images make clear that the key differences between the formal development of skyscrapers in the two cities resulted from different typical sites and municipal codes. No matter the hometown of the architect, the *genius loci* made the Flatiron a typical Manhattan tower.

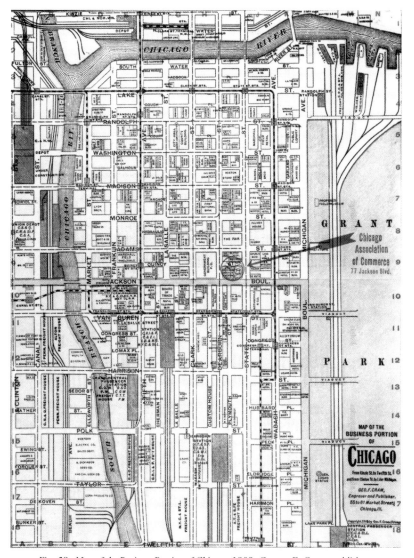

Fig. 39 *Map of the Business Portion of Chicago*, 1909. George F. Cram, publisher.

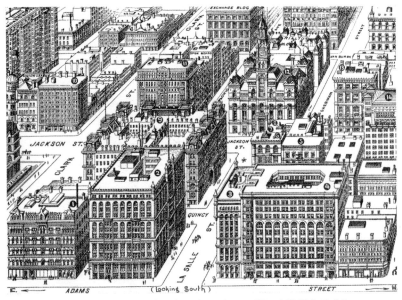

Fig. 40 Vicinity of Board of Trade, with Rookery and Rand-McNally Buildings, both court buildings, in foreground. Rand-McNally map, 1898.

Chicago to 1923

"If you look at our streets, you will find that the typical building of Chicago is the hollow square type," asserted architect George C. Nimmons to the Zoning Committee of the Chicago Real Estate Board in 1922.[26] He was referring to the many structures erected from the late 1880s through the 1910s with a large central light court—for example, the Rookery, Masonic Temple, Rand-McNally, Railway Exchange, and Peoples Gas, among others. These atrium buildings did not constitute the majority of Loop highrises simply because most lots were too small for such a plan, but they did represent the characteristic solution for prestige properties. They were the equivalents of major Manhattan towers. *(Fig. 40)*

In Chicago, as in New York, the city's historic mapping and municipal regulations were the two salient factors affecting the formal development of tall office buildings and the central business district. Platted in the 1830s, the city was laid out with large, squarish blocks of about 360 x 320 feet and streets 66 or 80 feet wide. Most blocks were bisected by an alley running either north-south or east-west, a public right-of-way that preserved some light and air on the interior of blocks and at the rear of many buildings. Roughly a square mile, this area was the city's business center and transit hub which became known as "the Loop," first for the cable cars, and then for the "El" that by 1900 ringed downtown. *(Fig. 39)* In the 1890s, there were numerous owners of parcels of a full quarter-block or larger—i.e., with at least one dimension of 160 feet. Smaller lots were sold as frontage and were generally 180 feet deep, as opposed to the 100-foot depth of half a block in the Manhattan grid. South of the Loop and near the railroad stations in the area between State and Pacific (now LaSalle) Streets, the grid changed proportions and was divided into long and narrow north-south blocks that afforded lots about seventy feet wide and of various lengths.[27]

A second influence was the more transient template of height controls, first levied in 1893. A real estate boom that began around 1888 had pushed the standard level of new office buildings to around 200 feet and had resulted in high vacancy rates that were rendered more serious by the financial panic of 1893. The concerns of the real estate industry, as well as of those who simply found the new buildings too tall, prompted the city council to set a limit on building heights of 130 feet. In the thirty years before the city passed a zoning law that permitted towers, the maximum height moved up and down between 130 and 260 feet.[28] At the same time, Manhattan towers stretched to 600 and 700 feet. While New York remained a frontier town where corporations and speculators pioneered new territories in the sky, the midwestern metropolis became a civilized landscape of regulated growth.

Until 1893, though, Chicago was a laissez-faire environment that outranked New York in both the number and height of its tall buildings. Speculators produced a dozen new office buildings ranging between sixteen and twenty stories, while New York had only four buildings of comparable height.[29] In the decade after the Home Insurance Building (1883–85), once considered the first office building with metal-frame and

Fig. 41 Aerial view, Michigan Boulevard, looking north, late 1910s.

curtain-wall construction, Chicago architects and engineers exploited the new technology.[30] Although the method was not embraced by all immediately, as the all-masonry Monadnock Building (1891) demonstrated, the appeal of economy as well as the advantages of admitting more light to interiors and keeping street-level windows large and the shops free of heavy columns, soon convinced conservatives.[31] In 1892, the twenty-story Masonic Temple rose 302 feet to the peak of its gabled roof, a height that tested the current limits of skeleton construction. Briefly the tallest building in the world, and the highest in the city by several stories, its altitude was an indulgence of its Masonic investors, whose lodges occupied the top four floors.[32] *(Fig. 42)*

More typical were the many sixteen- or seventeen-story buildings that sprang up between 1888 and 1895; permits for these projects were filed before height restrictions were imposed, and construction began several years later. These included the Manhattan, Marquette, Old Colony, Fisher

Figs. 42, 43 Masonic Temple (1892), Monadnock Addition Building (1893).

(Fig. 44), Monadnock Addition *(Fig. 43)*, Ashland, and Unity Buildings, among others. All of these were speculative projects erected by individuals or by stock subscription purely as rental properties. They were not company headquarters or celebrations of ego; indeed, some owners, such as the Boston brothers, Peter and Shepherd Brooks, never even visited their buildings.[33]

Factors that constrained height in Chicago's laissez-faire period included the engineering limits of steel-cage construction and of the caisson foundations that were necessary in the city's muddy, unstable soil. These figured in the calculations of the economic height of Chicago highrises, which was about sixteen or seventeen stories. In 1893, however, the city capped cornices at 130 feet, or about ten stories. This ceiling moved up and down several times in response to pressures from the real estate industry: in 1902 it went up to 260 feet, but was reduced to 200 in 1911, then in 1920 was again raised to 264.[34] Thus, after 1893, Chicago

Figs. 44, 45 Fisher Building, Reliance Building (both 1895).

engineers' expertise for vertical construction greatly exceeded the number of stories allowed by law.

The historical grid, the programmatic limitation for shallow, well-lit offices, and, after 1893, height restrictions produced two characteristic solutions for Chicago office buildings. The first was a solid, rectangular form, either tall and thin, like the Reliance Building *(Fig. 45)*, or high and long, like the Monadnock *(Fig. 43)*; the second type was a light-court building—either a cube-like block with a "hollow square," a "U" plan, or other variations. *(Figs. 54–71)*

The first type was more common at the southern end of the Loop where the city's grid of large square units switched to long narrow north-south blocks approximately 70 x 400 feet. *(Fig. 46)* Many of the early sky-scrapers of the Chicago School occupied these blocks, including the Manhattan (on a lot 68 x 150 feet), Old Colony (68 x 148 feet), and Fisher Buildings (70 x 100 feet).[35] Because they occupied the full width of

Fig. 46 Rand-McNally Map, 1898, showing Printing-House Row.
Note Old Colony and Manhattan Buildings, upper left.

the block, these buildings had excellent light and views onto streets, rather than onto alleys or rear courts. The seventy-foot width was perfectly suited for a plan with a double-loaded corridor—two rows of offices about twenty-five feet deep on either side of a generous central circulation space. As in New York buildings, the elevators and services could be efficiently grouped in a compact core. This arrangement can be seen in the plans of the Old Colony and Monadnock Addition Buildings. *(Figs. 47, 48)* Erected in sections, the Monadnock filled an entire block (68 x 420 feet); the efficiency of its plan produced an impressive ratio of sixty-eight percent rentable area.[36]

In the heart of the Loop, during the time that height was unrestricted, a few tall, thin buildings occupied lots small enough that they could take advantage of a compact core. The Reliance Building (1891/1895) rose fourteen stories on a corner lot 56 x 85 feet, and the Schiller Building (1892) ingeniously developed a mid-block lot with a combined theater and

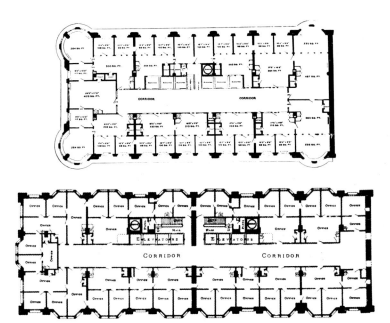

Figs. 47, 48 Typical floor plans, Old Colony Building (1894)
and Monadnock Addition Building (1893).

office building with a street facade of only 80 feet, and a depth of 180
feet.[37]

For lots wider than seventy or eighty feet, however, light courts were
necessary to provide adequate sunlight and air to interiors. For the largest
sites—that is, of around a quarter of a block or more—the hollow square,
also called the "O" plan, offered the most logical and profitable arrangement. Such lots were quite common: a map of the central business district
in 1909 showed over forty buildings that occupied a site of a full quarter
block.[38] There were two variations of this scheme: offices could be placed
either in a single outer ring with circulation on the interior court, or
aligned along a double-loaded corridor with both an outer and an inner
ring of suites. The first plan offered a poor ratio of rental to public space.
The second could increase the office area on each floor by fifty percent or
more, and so was preferred by developers if the site was sufficiently
large.[39]

Figs. 49, 50 Chamber of Commerce Building (1888–90).
View and interior court.

The first scheme was more common in earlier structures such as the Chamber of Commerce Building (on a lot 185 x 95 feet) or the Masonic Temple (170 x 114 feet). Their courts were soaring atriums covered by a glass skylight at roof level and ringed with a lacework of iron railings. In the thirteen-story Chamber of Commerce Building (1888–90), the space was narrow, only 35 x 108 feet, but 200 feet high; this slot was described in a city guidebook as admitting "a perfect flood of light [that] penetrates the central court so that the interior of the building is almost as brightly illuminated as the exterior during the day."[40] *(Figs. 49, 50)*

At the Masonic Temple, the enclosed court ascended the full twenty stories in an architectural *tour de force*. The primary function of the space was to bring light and ventilation into the center of the attenuated block and to the more than 200 offices that occupied floors ten through sixteen. The plan changed on these upper floors; rather than a ring of open corridors and ornate balconies, an inner ring of offices walled the court with windows. Many of these rooms were quite small, only 9 x 11 feet;

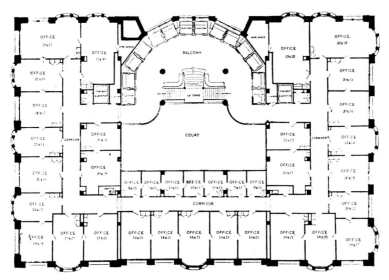

Fig. 51 Masonic Temple (1892).
Plan of tenth through sixteenth floors.

there were also larger suites of 500 to 600 square feet. *(Fig. 51)* On the lower floors, the developers planned a vertical mall (to use a modern term). Although retail space was common in lobbies, on second-floor balconies, and for lower-level restaurants, nine floors of stores were unprecedented, and apparently too ambitious: the venture failed after three years.[41]

More popular than the full-height atrium was a two-story court ringed with shops or services and glazed to admit natural light. In one of the earliest and most impressive, the 1888 Rookery, the lobby led to a large central court enveloped by a canopy of glass and filigree cast iron. *(Fig. 52)* Balcony suites were reached by a grand marble staircase that was the centerpiece of the space. The same general scheme, though developed in a more restrained neoclassical manner, was used in the 1903 Railway Exchange, the 1912 Insurance Exchange, and the 1915 Conway Building. Above the glass roof, the interior court was open to the sky, and the walls were faced with pale glazed brick to reflect light.

Fig. 52 Rookery Building (1888). Frank Lloyd Wright renovation of interior court (1905).

Another common scheme for the court was to develop a commercial arcade on the full ground floor, especially where it offered through-block traffic, and to use the second floor for a grand, vaulted, or skylit banking hall or trading floor, as in the Illinois Continental and Commercial Bank, or Illinois Merchants Bank. In the 1911 Peoples Gas Company Building, the upper-level columned atrium allowed customers to pay their bills in imperial splendor.[42] *(Fig. 53)*

The lavish architectural treatment of internal courts was an important aspect of the economic equation of Chicago's large office buildings. Shops yielded much higher rents than offices; one expert estimated that in New York's financial district the rate for retail was five to six times that for the office space above it.[43] In Chicago, as in all American cities except New York, the land values for retail use were higher than for office buildings, as is discussed in Part II. Thus the ground-floor stores with their large windows and entrances on the street, as well as the shops or showrooms in the atrium, comprised a substantial part of a building's revenues. The historian Daniel Bluestone has discussed the richness of these spaces as

Fig. 53 Peoples Gas Company Building (1911), customer room.

manifestations of the cultural aspirations of the buildings' owners and the desire to define office workers as a professional class.[44] Clearly, though, these quasi-public spaces were, first and foremost, a commercial strategy.

From around the turn of the century through the 1910s, the dominant approach for major office buildings was the massive palazzo type erected throughout the Loop, in particular by the firm of Daniel H. Burnham, and its successor, Graham, Anderson, Probst and White. Some examples included the Railway Exchange, First National Bank, Peoples Gas, Illinois Continental and Commercial Bank, Conway, and Insurance Exchange Buildings. *(Figs. 54–59)* Their classical character registered the influence of the Columbian Exposition, Burnham, and the 1909 *Plan of Chicago*, and reflected a Progressive Era desire for civic image and order. Facades were composed in a tripartite division: a heavy base of several stories, a middle section of identical office floors, and an upper zone of three or four stories, articulated by a colonnade or other ornament and capped by a cornice. Masonry, brick, or glazed terra-cotta clothed the exterior walls with varying degrees of decoration. The heights of these structures

Figs. 54–57 Chicago quarter-block buildings.
Top: Railway Exchange Building (1903), First National Bank Building (1896).
Bottom: Peoples Gas Company Building (1911), Illinois Continental and Commercial
Bank Building (1914).

Figs. 58–61 Chicago quarter-block buildings.
Top: Insurance Exchange Building (1912 and 1928), Conway Building (1915).
Bottom: Illinois Merchants Bank Building (1924), Builders' Building (1927).

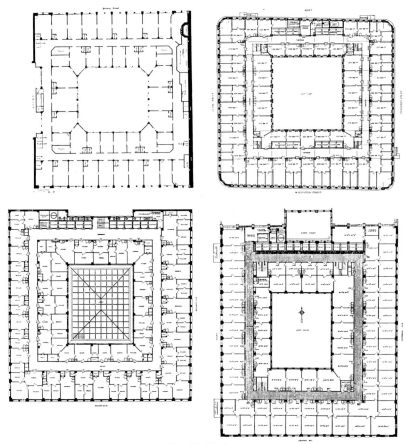

Figs. 62–65 Plans.
Top: Rand-MacNally Building (1890), Conway Building (1915).
Bottom: Railway Exchange Building (1915), Peoples Gas Company Building (1911).
plans are not shown at the same scale

ranged from sixteen to twenty stories, depending on the building code's limit during the year that plans were filed.

These buildings occupied large plots and thus were developed with a hollow-square plan with two rings of offices: perimeter and inner court.[45] This solution appeared in the late 1880s in the Rand-McNally Building (on a lot 125 x 171 feet, with an internal court 60 x 67 feet) *(Fig. 62)* and in the Rookery (177 x 168 feet with a court 62 x 71 feet), among others. It became a standard layout in the early twentieth century; illustrated here are the plans of the Peoples Gas Company, on a site 196 x 171 feet, and Conway Buildings (200 x 205 feet), and the Railway Exchange Building (171 x 172 feet). *(Figs. 63–65)* The double-loaded corridor afforded good plan efficiency and well-lit offices. Although the hollow-square plan had some disadvantages—in particular, the distance of some offices from the elevators—overall, it was a productive plan for the medium-height buildings allowed by the municipal restrictions. Indeed, it survived into the twenties, even after the zoning law permitted towers, in buildings such as the Illinois Merchants Bank *(Fig. 60)*, the Federal Reserve Bank, and the Builders' Building *(Fig. 61)*, among others.

The dominant aesthetic for office buildings in Chicago was to appear as big as possible by rising as a sheer wall above the sidewalks. Rarely did an architect place a light court in the street facade, as in the H-plan of New York's Equitable Building.[46] Even when a site was substantial, though perhaps not large enough to require an inner court, the building often posed as a palazzo-like cube. This approach can be seen in the U-shaped plan of the Marquette Building (115 x 190 feet) or in the McCormick Building (172 x 101 feet), which was constructed in two phases, the south section in 1910, the north in 1912. *(Figs. 66–69)* With the light court at the rear of the lot, often abutting the public alley, the "U" was a very efficient plan.[47] The open side allowed more light to enter the court throughout the day and saved the high costs of another exterior wall. For tenants, this plan offered better access to elevators and allowed companies leasing a half or full floor to close off corridors, leaving public areas only near the elevators.[48] The "U" plan was chosen by some owners even when the site was

Figs. 66, 67 Marquette Building (1895). View and plan.

large enough to warrant an interior court, as in the Commercial National Bank (180 x 190 feet). *(Figs. 70, 71)* For smaller lots, there were other variations in the position of the light court, such as an "L," which was common for corner lots.

In New York, the city of towers, prestige came with height. In Chicago, where after 1893 height was constrained, major office buildings impressed with imposing mass. In shaping the formal solutions for characteristic Chicago highrises in the first two decades of the twentieth century, as important as aesthetic ideals or the influence of leading architects were the actions of the city government and the real estate industry to protect

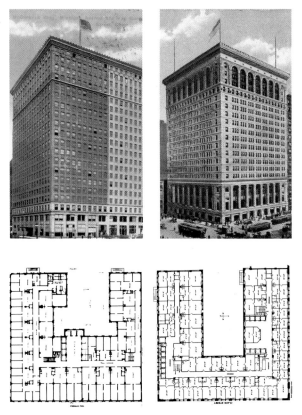

Figs. 68–71 McCormick Building, constructed in two campaigns (1910 and 1912), and Commercial National Bank (1895). Views and plans.

against overbuilding by limiting building height. Together, municipal regulations and the city's historic plat of large square blocks generated the Chicago vernacular—a big, boxy building penetrated at the center or rear by a large light court.

Fig. 72 Cities Service Building (1931).
Photo illustrates constructed zoning envelope with and without tower.

New York: Zoning and the Setback Style

The passage in 1916 of New York's first zoning legislation changed the rules of the game for skyscraper design. In addition to regulating uses by districts (commercial, residential, and unrestricted), the law limited the height and bulk of tall buildings with a formula called the *zoning envelope*. Designed to protect some measure of light and air for Manhattan's canyons, it required that after a maximum vertical height above the side-walk (usually 100 or 125 feet) a building must be stepped back as it rose in accordance with a fixed angle drawn from the center of the street. A tower of unlimited height was permitted over one-quarter of the site. The result-ing "setback" or "wedding cake" massing, with or without a tower, became the characteristic form for the New York skyscraper from the 1920s through the 1950s.[49] *(Fig. 72)*

The concept of the zoning envelope was entirely new. Rather than a flat cap on height as in Chicago, the New York law established a three-dimensional template. *(Fig. 75)* Before the ordinance, an owner could build straight up into the stratosphere. After 1916, height was still unre-stricted on one quarter of the lot, but on three quarters of the lot, both bulk and form were regulated, at least as a maximum. The New York law thus imposed restrictions on seventy-five percent of the property, while leaving twenty-five percent inviolate. Compared with the laissez-faire years, the degree of regulation was substantial. This compromise code continued to allow very dense development in prime areas, especially in the late twen-ties when skyscrapers regularly climbed to fifty and sixty stories or higher, and by mid-decade many were criticizing the ordinance as too liberal. In 1916, though, after more than twenty years of failed efforts to limit tall buildings, New York's zoning was a landmark event.[50]

Through the early twentieth century, the conditions zoning sought to allay—extreme density of coverage, congestion, lack of sunlight and fresh air on streets and inside buildings, and fears for public health and safety, especially in the event of fire—had become a serious problem. In the finan-cial district, taller and taller buildings crammed together, multiplying the area of their lots up to thirty times or more and casting neighbors into permanent shadow. A photo from around 1915 showed the American Surety Building, which twenty years before had reigned over Broadway, now dwarfed by the Equitable Building and other towers. *(Fig. 73)*

Urban reformers and City Beautiful advocates had been promoting a limit on building heights since the 1890s. Prominent architects such as Thomas Hastings recommended a maximum of eight or ten stories. In 1896, Ernest Flagg, who later designed the Singer Building, outlined a plan that both regulated the height and bulk of buildings according to a formula geared to the width of the street and limited a tower to one quarter of the site. Flagg's plan, which was a precedent for the 1916 ordinance, was praised in the press but failed to find political support. From 1906 to 1908, another effort to control heights by revising the building code was waged, but again the proposals failed to be implemented. Although there was greater sympathy at City Hall after 1909, when Fusion mayor William J. Gaynor and Manhattan Borough President George P. McAneny took office, reformers could not force legislation without the backing of business and real estate interests.[51]

That support finally began to materialize between 1911 and 1913 and led directly to the drafting of the ordinance in 1913 and its passage in 1916. A major reason for this shift was widespread concern for maintaining property values.[52] The real estate industry was in recession in 1913; after record activity in conveyances and construction in 1905 and 1906, construction dropped sharply during the financial panic of 1907. Another banner year in 1909 saw the largest number of building plans ever filed in the borough of Manhattan, yet this burst was followed by a slow, steady decline. In January 1915, the *Real Estate Record and Builders Guide* reported that the previous two years had been a time of "unprecedented stagnation" and that prospects for recovery were uncertain.[53] Vacancies in highrise buildings south of Chambers Street averaged 12.5 percent in 1913, with rates for the second through sixth floors running from 15 to 17 percent. Given these conditions of oversupply, building owners and developers began to favor zoning restrictions on new construction.[54]

Fig. 73 Skyscrapers of Lower Manhattan, c.1915.
Equitable Building at center, American Surety Building behind spire of Trinity Church.

In this regard, the Equitable Building has often been cited as the structure that "was a final cause of the zoning law."[55] But as historian Sally Chappell has shown, that skyscraper was a hole in the ground in 1913 when the Heights of Buildings Commission drafted the ordinance, and was completed in 1915, that is, when the political support for the law was solid.[56] Nevertheless, the enormous structure did become a lightning rod for criticism. A monotonous limestone wall nearly 200 feet long and 542 feet high, it cut off many views to the harbor, while shading prime property for some four blocks to its north. The design was treated by the press as the paragon example of greedy, overscaled development. The Equitable multiplied the area of its lot some thirty times, whereas the formula proposed by the new zoning allowed only about twelve times the lot area.

More important, though, than the public or professional critique of its exterior of form was the insistent fact of its vast interior space—1.2 million square feet. Before the steel was set, the developers had opened a leasing office and started an aggressive marketing campaign, and although the

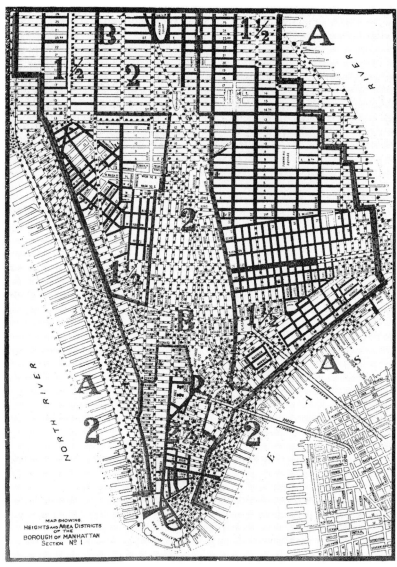

Fig. 74 1916 Zoning map, showing height (numbers)
and use (letters) districts in lower Manhattan.

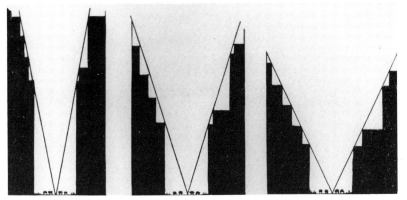

Fig. 75 Zoning diagrams, three height districts.

building did not fill up immediately, it did succeed in stealing tenants as well as sunlight from surrounding buildings.[57] As a result, many owners requested and were granted reductions in tax assessments, a situation that greatly concerned city officials.[58] In ways that touched many interests, the Equitable Building demonstrated the vulnerability of the business district to continued unregulated development and broadened the support for zoning.

Passed by the City's Board of Estimate on July 25, 1916, the zoning ordinance applied the principle of the zoning envelope to all commercial highrises, whether office buildings, light manufacturing lofts, or residential hotels (though not to apartment houses until a change in the Multiple Dwellings Law in 1929).[59] There were five formulas based on the width of the street and the angle of the setback. These were described as "districts," which referred to the height of the maximum vertical wall above the street permitted in that area.[60] *(Figs. 74, 75)* For example, in a "1 1/2 times district," where the street was 100 feet wide, the building could rise sheer 150 feet before the first setback. Above that level, the mass had to step back in a ratio of 1:3, i.e., one foot back for each three feet of additional height. On a 100-foot wide street in a "2 times district," the facade could reach 200 feet before it began stepping back at the rate of 1:4. The five formulas produced numerous permutations since

Figs. 76, 77 Paramount Building (1927) and 120 Wall Street (1930).

both the width of streets and the factor of multiplication varied. In general, buildings on avenues could rise sheer for about fourteen to eighteen floors; on side streets, nine to twelve stories before the first setback was common.

The zoning envelope had several important effects on skyscraper design and development. If owners wanted to exploit the maximum volume allowed for the lot, the shape of the building was, in effect, predesigned by the code. The limit of the envelope was defined by a diagonal plane, but since diagonals were ill-suited to steel-cage construction, the practice was to step back the mass at regular intervals that usually related to the depth of the structural bay. In a district with a ratio of 1:3, for example, after a twelve-foot recession, there could be another vertical rise of thirty-six feet before the next setback, the equivalent of three floors; a sixteen-foot setback allowed a vertical of forty-eight feet, or about four floors, etc. The multiple steps of the upper stories of the Paramount

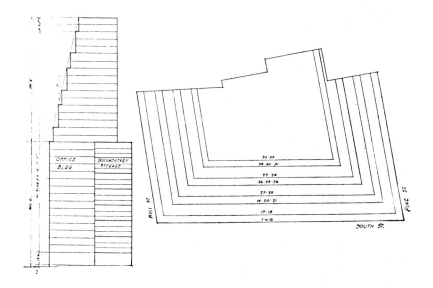

Fig. 78 120 Wall Street zoning diagrams from office of architect, Ely Jacques Kahn.

Building at Times Square or 120 Wall Street show how owners and architects squeezed the maximum from the zoning envelope.[61] *(Figs. 76–78)* These ziggurat-like structures did not develop the option for a tower, which was often the case on middle-sized lots. Because towers were expensive to build, many developers preferred more economical structures that offered a good rate of return without higher risks. In prime areas with high rents, though, towers were standard. The Lincoln, Chanin, French, and General Electric Buildings and 500 Fifth Avenue all capitalized on proximity to Grand Central. *(Figs. 79, 80, 82–84)* The Bank of Manhattan Company, Irving Trust/1 Wall Street, and City Bank Farmers Trust crowded towers of fifty to seventy stories into the congested financial district. *(Figs. 81, 85, 86)* Symmetry and visual balance were architectural ideals often sacrificed for additional rents, especially in buildings that fronted on two streets governed by different envelopes, as illustrated by the asymmetrical massing of most of the buildings shown here.

Figs. 79–82 Zoning envelope towers, New York.
Top: Lincoln Building (1930), Chanin Building (1928).
Bottom: Bank of Manhattan (1930), General Electric Building (1931).

Figs. 83–86 Zoning envelope towers, New York.
Top: French Building (1927), 500 Fifth Avenue (1931).
Bottom: Irving Trust/1 Wall Street (1931), City Bank Farmers Trust (1931).

Fig. 87 Chanin Building (1928) and Chrysler Building (1930).

The zoning formula also encouraged larger buildings. The unlimited height permitted on one quarter of the site made large lots particularly attractive, since they allowed for taller, more profitable towers. Because much of the space inside a tower is consumed by elevator shafts and other service areas, at least 100 x 200 feet was needed to make a tower of fifty stories practicable. The Bank of Manhattan Company crammed seventy floors onto an irregular Wall Street lot of about 150 x 200 feet. *(Fig. 81)* In midtown, the seventy-story Chrysler Building occupied a site 200 x 205 feet, and had tower floors with up to 8,800 square feet. *(Figs. 87, 90)* The enormity of the Empire State Building's site, 197 x 425 feet, meant that its tower could expand to 100 x 212 feet; this afforded upper floors with about 15,000 square feet of rentable space.[62] *(Fig. 96)* Thus, both the logic of the zoning envelope and the economics of development argued for big buildings on large sites.

Some developers did try to pack tall buildings onto smaller parcels. At the busy corner of Fifth Avenue and Forty-second Street, fifty-nine stories were piled onto a lot measuring only 100 x 208 feet, half the area of the Chrysler Building; the tower floors of 500 Fifth Avenue contained up to 4,500 square feet. *(Figs. 84, 89)* The thirty-eight-story Fred French Building, on Fifth Avenue at Forty-fifth Street, occupied a lot only 79 x 200 feet and had tower floors of only 1,500 to 3,000 square feet. *(Figs. 83, 88)* In comparison, in 1912, Bankers Trust had squeezed about the same number of stories onto a site half the size. An article in *The American Architect* in 1930 noted that the French Building was among the first to show "the economic possibilities of a tower on a lot that was not, at that time, considered large enough," and that "the subsequent construction of two more towers next to it along the avenue prove the soundness of the policy."[63] These buildings demonstrate how the equation of *form follows finance* was always searching for new proofs for its changing variables.

Zoning also affected the aesthetics of skyscraper design. By the mid-1920s, a number of architects and critics were writing about a new design approach that some labeled the "setback style." The term *style* is used in this study with reservations; nevertheless, a new aesthetic clearly had evolved from the requirements of the zoning law.[64] The change began around 1922, when architect Harvey Wiley Corbett and delineator Hugh Ferriss began to publish articles and drawings on the potential influence of zoning. Around 1923–1924, several new skyscrapers had turned the requirements of the zoning formula to advantage by reducing the number of setbacks and emphasizing the power of the pyramidal mass; in particular, the Shelton Hotel and the Barclay-Vesey Telephone Building were lauded by critics who found beauty in their monumental scale and simplified silhouette. These buildings helped to popularize an aesthetic of simple,

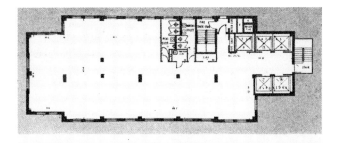

FRENCH BUILDING

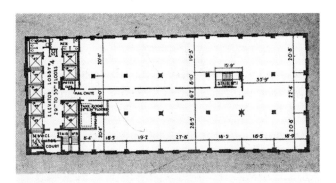

LINCOLN BUILDING

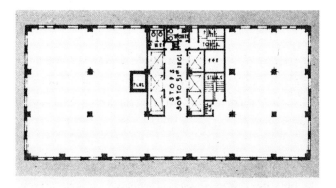

CHANIN BUILDING

Fig. 88 Three tower floor plans: French Building (1927) 29th–34th floors, Lincoln Building (1930) 23rd–47th floors, Chanin Building (1928) 32nd–51st floors.

sculptural mass that became the benchmark of progressive design by the mid-twenties.[65] Ely Jacques Kahn, one of the most prolific skyscraper designers of the period, observed: "The New York zoning laws protecting property rights, light, and air have encouraged a new art by reason of the very restrictions they contain."[66]

"Finance Dictates the Fenestration; Rent Rolls Rule the *Parti*"

In contrast to earlier periods when the best descriptions and analysis of the practical aspects of office building design were offered by professional writers such as Barr Ferree and George Hill, the most incisive discussions of the highrise to appear in the professional press in the twenties were written by the skyscraper architects themselves. These articles gave little attention to facade treatment or other points of style, but focused instead on issues of plan and program as they determined form. The fundamentals of layout were not much changed from those described earlier, but it is interesting to hear them articulated by practicing architects rather than by developers, building managers, or other professionals of the real estate industry. The purpose of these articles may have been in part for the architects to establish their credentials as experts. It seems, though, that one motive was to help colleagues comprehend that office building design had an intrinsic logic that had best be followed to produce a successful building.

Several articles, for example, described how skyscrapers must be designed from the inside out, from the top down, and from the smallest room to the larger whole. As Corbett explained in a 1924 article in *The Architectural Forum*:

> The usual procedure in most plan studies is to start with the ground floor
> and build up. But in planning office buildings, one must reverse this
> process and start from the top and build down. That is to say, one devel-
> ops a typical upper floor plan first, because there are a large number of
> typical upper floors to one ground floor. The major income is from these

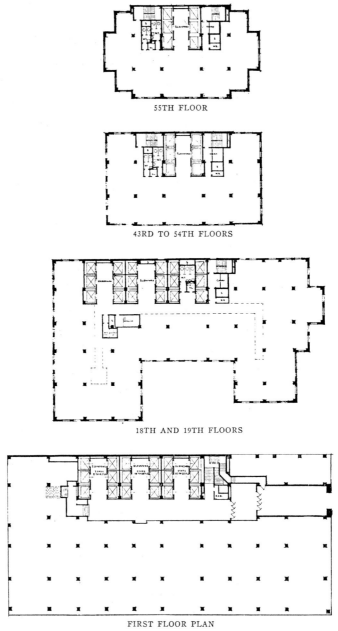

55TH FLOOR

43RD TO 54TH FLOORS

18TH AND 19TH FLOORS

FIRST FLOOR PLAN

Fig. 89 Floor plans, 500 Fifth Avenue (1931).

typical floors, and if some sacrifice in plan arrangement is to be made, it might be better made once on the ground floor than to be repeated twenty or thirty times on typical floors. In the same way, and for the same reason, the typical floor must be planned on the basis of the typical office unit. So one first plans this unit, then one strings several of these along both sides of a corridor, then places the necessary line of vertical circulation at a central point off the corridor making sure that no unfortunate tenant has to walk over 100 feet.[67]

Emphasizing the primacy of the interior layout, Walter Kilham, Jr., who was employed in the office of Raymond Hood, observed in a 1930 article in *The American Architect*: "The frame of building should not be designed from the point of view of the most practical engineering, but from the standpoint of what the space it encloses is to be used for."[68] Similarly, one of the architects of the Empire State Building, R. H. Shreve, quipped: "Finance dictates the fenestration; rent rolls rule the *parti*."[69]

There was a great deal of consensus about the best dimensions for the standard office unit, which was generally about nine feet wide and twenty to thirty feet deep. Arthur Loomis Harmon noted that in order to permit the greatest flexibility, "a nine-foot wide office is considered most desirable by the greatest number of tenants, so that the column spacing is determined at about eighteen feet, and the fenestration becomes a series of windows, each from four to five feet wide and from six to seven feet high, about nine feet on center."[70] A 1925 study by the National Association of Building Owners and Managers (NABOM) confirmed this point, showing that a nine-foot width would accommodate the layout of eighty-two percent of all private offices in the several cities surveyed.[71] Detroit architect Albert Kahn favored a somewhat smaller unit of eight feet with structural bays of sixteen and a half to seventeen feet.[72] Opinion varied somewhat on the optimal depth for office space. Corbett defined the best office space in terms of light: "The depth of a well-lighted office is never over twice the clear ceiling height, and twenty feet is far better than twenty-five."[73]

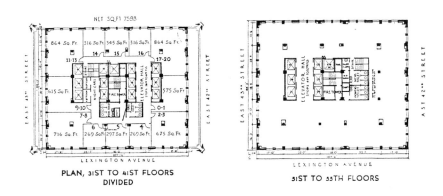

NET SQ.FT. 7593

PLAN, 31ST TO 41ST FLOORS DIVIDED

31ST TO 55TH FLOORS

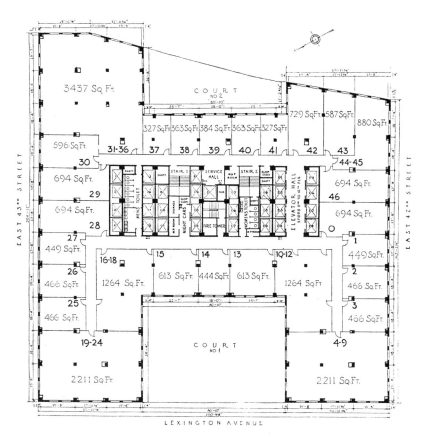

PLAN, 6TH TO 10TH FLOORS, DIVIDED

Fig. 90 Floor plans, Chrysler Building (1930).

note scale change in tower plans

In "The Economic Design of Office Buildings," R. H. Shreve described how the typical office unit in New York (approximately twenty feet wide and twenty-five to thirty feet deep) could be divided into two small offices of nine to ten feet, each with a window "perhaps 4'6" or 5'0" wide," and with an anteroom or work space opening onto the public corridor.[74] These standard units could be lined up along both sides of a corridor six or seven feet wide to produce an efficient and well-lit plan: this arrangement can be seen in the tower section of the Lincoln Building, or in a variation on an "H" plan, as in the middle sections of the Chrysler Building. *(Fig. 90)* It is notable that at least three floor plans cut at different levels of the building are needed to explain the form of a New York setback, whereas in the earlier periods in both Chicago and New York, as well as in Chicago in the twenties, most tall buildings could be described either by one plan of a typical floor or by two plans, one of the base and another of the tower section.

The arrangement of the core—the elevators, services, and circulation—depended on the size of the site and its location, on whether it was a corner or mid-block lot, and on the presence of neighboring structures or the main direction of pedestrian traffic. For small- or medium-sized lots there was more variation, since the position of the core had to be adapted to renting strategies, such as the ease of subdividing office suites or the potential to lease full floors.[75] This was the case, for example, at the French and Lincoln Buildings, and at 500 Fifth Avenue, where the elevators were placed at the far end of the lobby. *(Figs. 88, 89)*

For larger sites that could support towers of adequate dimensions, the optimal arrangement was a full perimeter of offices encircling a central core, as seen in the Chrysler and Empire State Buildings. *(Figs. 90, 96)* Because tower space commanded the highest office rents per square foot, the position of the elevators on upper floors affected the plan of all lower stories. As Corbett explained, where several banks of elevators were required "the problem becomes one of two buildings, one placed on top of the other, with the vertical circulation of the top building running through the lower as an "express" service."[76] The challenge to the architect

TABLE No. 10

BUILDING COST PER SQUARE FOOT OF NET RENTABLE AREA BY CHIEF COMPONENT FACTORS

Component Factors	8 Stories	15 Stories	22 Stories	30 Stories	37 Stories	50 Stories	63 Stories	75 Stories
Excavations and Foundations	$0.738	$0.476	$0.399	$0.413	$0.435	$0.438	$0.449	$0.415
Structural Steel	0.717	0.798	0.869	0.952	1.009	1.151	1.351	1.726
Concrete Floors	0.608	0.580	0.575	0.572	0.583	0.603	0.625	0.642
Permanent Interior Partitions	0.224	0.233	0.256	0.274	0.286	0.321	0.356	0.386
Brickwork	0.177	0.252	0.324	0.369	0.410	0.471	0.515	0.551
Exterior Finish	0.397	0.497	0.515	0.531	0.517	0.508	0.506	0.515
Roofing	0.060	0.057	0.048	0.040	0.037	0.036	0.032	0.030
Windows and Glazing	0.191	0.183	0.195	0.201	0.209	0.221	0.230	0.239
Interior Finish and Trim	1.821	1.746	1.785	1.804	1.803	1.848	1.894	1.910
Mechanical Equipment	1.765	1.813	2.054	2.423	2.699	2.975	3.269	3.623
(a) Elevators and Elevator Fronts	0.614	0.651	0.868	0.926	1.104	1.245	1.408	1.656
(b) Plumbing, Drainage and Water Supply	0.434	0.500	0.532	0.567	0.641	0.667	0.717	0.765
(c) Electric Light and Power, Wiring, etc.	0.269	0.305	0.323	0.352	0.364	0.384	0.402	0.419
(d) Heating and Ventilating	0.448	0.356	0.331	0.578	0.590	0.679	0.742	0.785
Tenants' Changes	0.594	0.662	0.68	0.700	0.701	0.699	0.693	0.688
Miscellaneous	0.397	0.286	0.244	0.309	0.280	0.256	0.238	0.227
Plant and General Conditions	0.481	0.425	0.414	0.429	0.436	0.448	0.467	0.492
Extras and Contingencies	0.230	0.224	0.223	0.218	0.217	0.218	0.220	0.219
Total Direct Labor and Material Cost	8.400	8.232	8.588	9.248	9.622	10.191	10.844	11.665
Total Building Cost	9.289	9.098	9.463	10.100	10.514	11.089	11.728	12.589
Land Cost ($200 Per Sq. Ft.)	31.553	20.172	16.467	13.695	12.335	10.863	9.798	9.041
Total Carrying Charges (Per Sq. Ft.)	2.384	1.925	1.907	1.926	1.999	2.055	2.148	2.284
Total Investment (Per Sq. Ft.)	43.226	31.195	27.837	25.921	24.847	24.008	23.674	23.913
Total Cost Assignable to Land	33.700	21.818	18.034	15.407	13.844	12.341	11.263	10.516
Total Cost Assignable to Building	9.526	9.377	9.803	10.514	11.003	11.667	12.411	13.397

Fig. 91 Building cost per square foot of net rentable area by chief component factors.

was to find the best layout for both sections. The pyramidal form dictated by the zoning envelope was in fact well-suited to the mechanical requirements of the building, since it utilized the otherwise unrentable deep spaces of the lower floors for elevator shafts and utility rooms. A well-designed core resulted in good "plan efficiency," which was the ratio of the net rentable space to the gross floor area. A plan was considered efficient if the area of rentable space was sixty-five to seventy percent of the gross floor area; in the Empire State Building, for example, the plan efficiency was 69:100.[77]

The average height of major New York office buildings increased through the twenties. Around 1925, large projects were generally between thirty to forty stories; by the end of the decade, the minimum height for a building with a tower in an area such as Wall Street or Grand Central was around forty to forty-five stories, even for lots as small as 11,000–12,000 square feet. Moreover, there were about a dozen skyscrapers taller than fifty floors, including four around seventy stories, and the Empire State, with eighty-five office floors.

The most profitable height for tall buildings was analyzed by a committee of architects, engineers, contractors, and building managers, and was published in 1930 as *The Skyscraper: A Study in the Economic Height of Modern Office Buildings*.[78] The authors were W. C. Clark, an economist and Vice President of S. W. Straus, a large mortgage bond company, and J. L. Kingston of the firm Sloan and Robertson, architects of the Chanin Building. They presented the experts' analysis of the relative costs of a series of eight office buildings ranging from eight to seventy-five stories. The hypothetical site was a corner lot south of Grand Central Terminal with the dimensions of 200 x 405 feet, that is, the full width of the block and about half to two-thirds of its area. They assumed a value of $200 per square foot for the site, which was considered conservative for the district. All the designs conformed to current zoning laws and building codes, and estimates of land and construction costs were based on current market rates.[79]

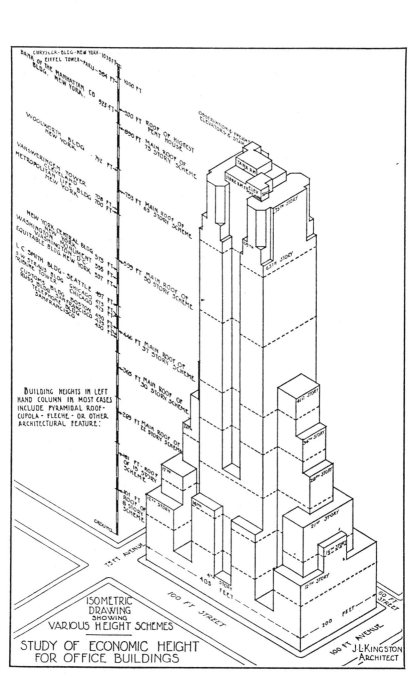

Fig. 92 Study of economic height for office buildings.

The team assayed a large number of tables, charts, and graphs that compared the relative costs of the eight alternative heights. The one reproduced here, Table 10, calculated the costs per square foot for chief component factors, including building materials, equipment, finishing, labor, financing, and land *(Fig. 91)*, and compared these to the net rentable area for each of the eight buildings. For example, the table showed that to produce one square foot of rentable space, the steel for a fifty-story building cost about $1.15, whereas for a seventy-five-story building, the same one foot cost $1.72 (due to the need to reinforce the weight of the additional stories). Except for land, costs rose moderately for each successively taller building.

Accompanying this data was a massing study that depicted the eight alternatives and gave a detailed description of the rationale for the various heights, all in a single image. *(Fig. 92)* As the authors explained:

In order to keep our comparison of the different buildings as closely as possible one of height, we used the same "parti" throughout, designing just one tall building and then reducing the height in various stages at the levels where the elevator banks terminated. This gave us a series of buildings designed with the same relative degree of efficiency, the only differences between them being logical variations due to changes in height. Seventy-five stories was taken as the maximum limit of our study because we originally believed that this point was well beyond the point of maximum economic return. To determine the point at which our next building would stop we eliminated the highrise elevators, which operate locally between the sixty-fourth and seventy-fifth stories and made the second building sixty-three stories high. Continuing this system of stepping down, we obtained a third building of fifty stories, a fourth of thirty-seven stories, a fifth of thirty stories, a sixth of twenty-two stories, a seventh of fifteen stories, and an eighth of eight stories. Study was given to the minimum height of eight stories because it has been seriously proposed in certain quarters that New York City should limit all buildings to a height of eight or ten stories.[80]

Of these options, the sixty-three-story building promised the highest rate of return. The experts calculated that a fifty-story building would return 9.87 percent, while seventy-five stories would produce 10.06 percent. Slightly better, though, was the 10.25 percent projected for the sixty-three-story structure. As Table 10 showed, increased construction costs of taller buildings were often offset by increased rents from additional stories. Clark and Kingston emphasized that only above sixty-three stories did the total cost assignable to the building exceed that of the land. A real estate rule of thumb held that land and building costs should be at least equal, although the value of the building was generally greater. The authors noted a basic rule: the higher the value of land, the taller a building must rise to reach the point of maximum economic return.[81]

In the overheated speculation of late 1920s, as land prices rose, towers grew steadily taller. Or should the order be: as skyscrapers grew taller, land prices rose? The variables that contributed to real estate cycles were even more complex than this "chicken and egg" conundrum. Another important factor driving up land prices was the easy availability of financing, as discussed in Part II.

The race skyward at the end of the "Roaring Twenties" did have a giddy aspect, as announcements of seventy-or-more-story skyscrapers became a frequent feature in the real estate news.[82] From 1931 to 1934, 26 million square feet of office space was completed in Manhattan. This staggering total added at the beginning of the Depression resulted in high vacancy rates and serious losses for many owners of new buildings. Given the large number of projects started in the late twenties, it seems difficult to fathom how individual developers and their bankers did not foresee the oversupply of office space that, in retrospect, seemed inevitable, but by examining one of these projects in detail, we can trace the step-by-step logic of the process.

Fig. 93 Empire State Building (1931).
compare with Fig. 92

89

The Empire State Example

The most colossal miscalculation of the 1920s was the Empire State Building, which remained three-quarters empty for a decade after its opening in 1931 and did not turn an annual profit until 1950.[83] The isolated tower at Thirty-fourth Street and Fifth Avenue remained the world's tallest building until the 1970s. *(Fig. 93)* Far from the clustered highrises near Grand Central, the Empire State was extraordinary in its size and siting, but was in every other way a standard speculative development. Excellent documentation exists for many aspects of the project, and this rich record allows us to see how economic considerations affected every aspect of its design. Indeed, because the site was so large, 197 x 425 feet, the building did not even fill the maximum zoning envelope on its lower floors. The Empire State demonstrated the principle of form follows finance better than most skyscrapers.

The men who erected and owned the Empire State Building did not originate the project. In 1928, an architect and developer, Floyd Brown, contracted to buy the famous but fading Waldorf-Astoria Hotel on Fifth Avenue and Thirty-fourth Street for $14,000,000, the highest price recorded in the city that year. In December, the *Real Estate Record and Builders Guide* published a rendering by the architects Shreve and Lamb Associates for a mixed-use building containing about 2,000,000 square feet of rental space with the lower twenty-five floors were devoted to shops and lofts and the top twenty-five to offices.[84] *(Fig. 94)* Through this publicity, Brown hoped to attract major tenants or investors whose commitments would help him meet his next $1.5 million mortgage payment; when these failed to materialize, he defaulted. Intrigued by the site, Brown's banker, Louis Kaufman, approached his longtime associates Pierre S. du Pont and John J. Raskob, two of the country's richest men. On August 28, 1929, Raskob sent a letter of understanding to Kaufman outlining their proposed participation.[85]

During these discussions, an important change of program was explored: transforming the project into a major office tower. Raskob's letter included a sheet of figures comparing the projected costs and income of

Waldorf - Astoria Hotel in the Year's Largest Sale

Celebrated Hostelry Is to Be Replaced by Fifty-Story Office Building
Representing Investment of Approximately $25,000,000

THE sale of the Waldorf-Astoria Hotel last week to the Bethlehem Engineering Corporation. Floyd Brown, President, by the Bloomer-du Pont interests indicates the rise of realty values in the Fifth Avenue-Thirty-fourth Street district. The owners of the famous hostelry no longer could resist the tide of rising values, Mr. Bloomer in his announcement saying:

"While the Waldorf-Astoria still maintains its world-wide prestige and an unimpaired volume of business, the great non-producing areas of the hotel, involving enormous taxation and operating costs, have become so burdensome, a more profitable use of the site than for hotel purposes is indicated. This is the reason for the sale."

The transaction represents the largest and most important sale of the year. There have been numerous other large transactions during 1928, but none approaches the Waldorf-Astoria transaction in either amount of money involved or in the magnitude of ground area. Nor does any other Manhattan project equal in ground area the proposed new building to be erected on the site, a fifty-story structure containing 2,000,000 square feet of rentable area and occupying 84,000 square feet.

While construction details of the new building are still being developed by Mr. Brown in association with the architects, Shreve & Lamb, and a number of managing and renting agents, the general plan as announced includes some unusual features. Chief among them are the vehicular ramps which will lead from Thirty-third and Thirty-fourth streets to a motor truck terminal in the basement of the building where trucks can be unloaded directly at the elevators. Another feature is a new street to be cut through the block between the building and the structure abutting on the west.

The new structure will occupy the 200-foot blockfront on Fifth Avenue and extend 425 feet west on Thirty-fourth and Thirty-third streets. It will be built in a series of setbacks for

(Continued on page 8)

Shreve & Lamb, Architects.
ARCHITECTS' SKETCH OF THE PROPOSED 50-STORY OFFICE BUILDING
TO BE ERECTED ON SITE OF WALDORF-ASTORIA HOTEL

Fig. 94 First proposal for fifty-story building on site of Empire State Building.

	55 Storeys		80 Storeys
Land - - - - - - - - - - - - - - -	$16,000,000	Land - - - - - - - - -	$16,000,000
29,000,000 cu ft. @ $1.00 - -- - - - -	29,000,000	34,000,000 cu. ft. @ $1.00 (25 addtl storeys 80 x 240	34,000,000
Total cost - - - - -	45,000,000		50,000,000
1st Mtg (5½% - 2% S.F.) - - - - - -	25,000,000		27,500,000
Balance - - - - - - - -	20,000,000		22,500,000
2nd Mtg (6½% with 20% of Com. Stk as bonus)	10,000,000		12,500,000
Balance - - - - - - -	10,000,000		10,000,000
Pfd. Srk (7% with 80% of Com.bonus)	10,000,000		10,000,000
INCOME			
1,750,000 sq. ft. @ $3.25 - - - - -	5,690,000	1,750,000 sq. ft. @ $3.25	5,690,000
		330,000 " " @ $4.00	1,310,000
			7,000,000
Vacancies 10 % - - - - - - - - -	570,000		700,000
	5,120,000		6,300,000
Op. Exp. 1,750,000 sq. ft. @ 75¢	1,312,500	2,080,000 Sq.Ft.@ 75¢	1,560,000
Taxes 40,000,000 " @ $2.66	1,047,500	44,000,000 " @$2.66	1,170,000
Total Expense - - -	2,360,000		2,730,000
Bal. for Capital - - - - - - - - -	2,760,000		3,570,000
1st Mortg. Interest - - - - - - - -	1,375,000		1,510,000
	1,385,000		2,060,000
1st Mtg. S. F. 2% - - - - - - - -	500,000		550,000
	885,000		1,510,000
2nd Mtg. Int - - - - - - - - - - -	650,000		810,000
Bal. for owners	235,000		700,000
$10,000,000 - 7% Pfd. Stk	700,000		700,000
Bal. for Com. Stk	465,000		0

2nd $12,500,000. $10,000,000
2,500,000
Pfd. $10,000,000.
$500,000

Fig. 95 Estimates for costs and income for fifty-five- and eighty-story variations of Empire State Building, August 1929.

two alternatives: fifty-five- and eighty-story buildings. *(Fig. 95)* The fifty-five-story scheme would contain 29,000,000 cubic feet, cost $45,000,000, and generate an income of $5,120,000—the equivalent of a gross return of 11.4 percent. The eighty-story building added 330,000 square feet of rentable space, producing an overall income of $6,300,000, and promised a gross return of 12.6 percent. Such numbers were persuasive arguments for greater height. The language of Raskob's letter, though, was guarded:

> Our present tentative feeling is that we should be able to build a building, the cubicle content of which will be about 34,000,000 feet at $1.00 per cubic foot including all charges of every kind such as interest, cost of demolition, architect and builder's commission, fees paid for securing mortgages, rental fees, etc. etc., which would mean a total cost of not more that $34,000,000, which added to the land cost of $16,000,000 would give a total cost of $50,000,000.[86]

Thus, through a series of small steps and tentative decisions, what had begun as a large, but unexceptional mixed-use structure was transformed into an enterprise that would capture the attention of the world. The project was was officially incorporated on September 5, 1929 as Empire State, Inc., and after that time the venture was all bombast and hyperbole.

How did the guidelines of 34 million cubic feet and $34 million translate into floor area and form? The industry rule of thumb used to render cubic feet into rentable floor area was 16:1, which meant that the Empire State Building would contain about 2.1 million square feet. The anticipated return on equity was determined by dividing the income from rents by the total costs, including construction, financing, taxes, overhead, etc.[87] The vexing variable in the equation was the estimated annual income from rents. In theory, one simply calculated how many square feet of rentable space could be constructed with the available budget, then multiplied that number by the average rental rate (less ten percent for vacancies). Repeating this formula for bigger and smaller buildings provided a means of comparing rates of return. Judging market rents was problematic,

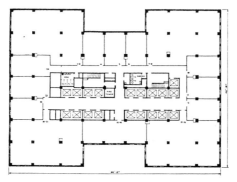

66TH AND 67TH FLOORS

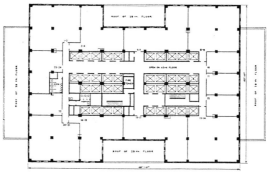

30TH AND 32ND; 40TH AND 43RD FLOORS

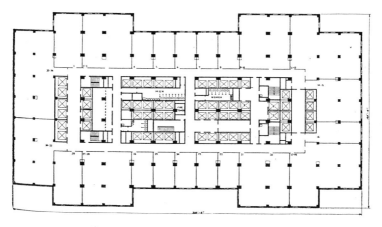

6TH TO 20TH FLOORS

Fig. 96 Empire State Building, typical floor plans.

94

though, since so many different factors could affect desirability. Given its size and its location outside of the popular office districts, the Empire State Building had no comparable model for guidelines.[88] The initial estimate of annual rent was $6,300,000, which, under the formula described, would have produced a gross return on equity of approximately 12.6 percent. In September 1930, around mid-point in construction, *Fortune* reported that the owners estimated their return would be about 10 percent. This was considered rather low for speculative development, although for a very tall building on high-priced land, it was about average.[89]

These initial estimates were based on standard real estate formulas, not on specific building plans. From the acquisition of the property in May 1929 until the formation of Empire State, Inc. in September, all plans had been *entirely financial, not architectural*. The different schemes were described only in numbers—stories, cubic feet, operating costs, and projected income. No drawings were included or referred to in these reports, and, indeed, Raskob's letter of intention noted that one of the next steps would be choosing architects to prepare a design.

Once the financial blueprint was in place, the owners hired a team of experts to generate the building program and plan, including architects, contractors, structural and mechanical engineers, elevator experts, and rental agents. The same firm that prepared Floyd Brown's initial fifty-story scheme, Shreve and Lamb (after 1929, Shreve, Lamb and Harmon) were selected as architects. The general contractors were Starrett Brothers and Eken, one of the country's largest builders and a company with a proven record of efficiency and speed in skyscraper construction.[90]

The guidelines developed by the team were described with perfect verbal economy in an article in *Architectural Forum* by William Lamb, the building's chief designer:

> The program was short enough—a fixed budget, no space more than twenty-eight feet from window to corridor, as many stories of such space as possible, an exterior of limestone, and completion date of May 1, 1931, which meant a year and six months from the beginning of the sketches.[91]

The first three criteria, he explained, determined the building's massing and height, the last two, the key features of the facade. Lamb also described how the owners' program translated directly into the building's internal arrangements and service core:

> The logic of the plan is very simple. A certain amount of space in the center, arranged as compactly as possible, contains the vertical circulation, toilets, shafts, and corridors. Surrounding this is a perimeter of office space twenty-eight feet deep. The sizes of the floors diminish as the elevators decrease in number....The four groups of high-rise elevators are placed in the center of the building with the low-rise groups adjoining on the east and west sides so that, as these drop off, the building steps back from the long dimension of the property to approach the square form of the shaft, with the result that instead of being a tower set upon a series of diminishing setbacks prescribed by the zoning law, the building becomes all tower rising from a great five-story base.[92]

The external form of the Empire State was thus a direct expression of the requirements of its interior layout. *(Figs. 96, 97)* The suites indicated on the typical floor plans represented possible subdivisions. Enclosure and partitioning of offices were finished after a specific area was rented.

Although zoning dictated that there be setbacks, their location at the twenty-first, twenty-fifth, and thirtieth floors was determined by economic factors. The maximum the lower section could have risen under the code was ten stories on Fifth Avenue and sixteen on Thirty-fourth Street; instead, after five stories, the mass set back a full sixty feet on the east and west sides. The resulting effect of a low base was praised by architectural critics for establishing a more human scale at the pedestrian level. The major reason for the setback, though, was to shield the lower-floor offices from the noise of the street, and to create a zone of sunlight and quiet that would bring higher rents. Setbacks below the thirtieth floor were also carved back to maintain the twenty-eight-foot maximum depth for first-class office space defined in the building program. At the base and top,

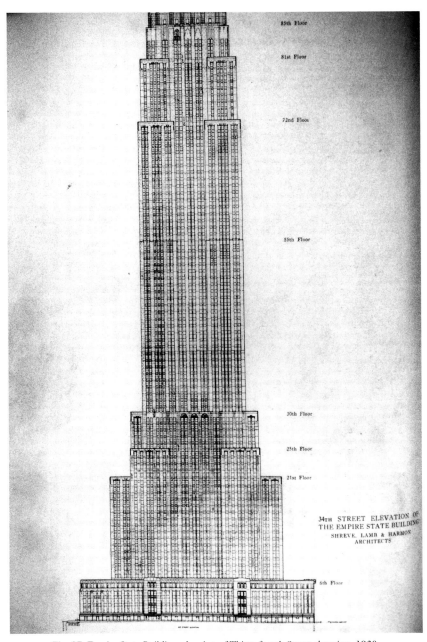

Fig. 97 Empire State Building, drawing of Thirty-fourth Street elevation, 1930.

Fig. 98 Empire State Building under construction, 1930.

then, market forces placed stricter limitations on the form of the building than did the zoning law.

Determining the height of the Empire State was a somewhat more complicated equation. The contemporary Clark and Kingston study (for which R. H. Shreve had been a consultant) calculated that the optimum height for a skyscraper on a site slightly smaller than that of the Empire State, but with comparable land costs, would be sixty-three stories. The height proposed in Raskob's first letter was eighty stories, but once hard estimates were made, the contractors reported that seventy-five stories would be the most economical height; to push the eighty-eight stories would require an additional bank of elevators. The decision to construct eighty-five stories involved some trade-offs. There was enormous advertising value in the title of "world's tallest" building, even if the extra floors

Fig. 99 Exterior construction of Empire State Building, 1930.

meant a slightly lower rate of return. The Chrysler's spire pointed at 1,048 feet, the height to beat. The owners therefore decided on eighty-five stories, 1,050 feet. When the directors weighed the costs of a less-than-profitable extra five or ten floors, the benefits of supreme height must have seemed worth the cost. In fact, the commercial office tower occupied only eighty floors, the top five floors were reserved for offices of the corporation directors and necessitated changing elevators, to those used for the observation deck.[93]

Early drawings showed the Empire State flat-topped. *(Fig. 97)* The revenue-raising tourist deck was planned in early schemes, but the "mooring mast"—supposedly for dirigibles, though the engineers knew that docking would be very problematic—was a later addition. The metal mast conveniently added 200 feet to the building's height, making it 1,250 feet (the equivalent of 102 stories), thus vanquishing challengers. As the directors had hoped, the observation deck did steal away the paying crowds from the Woolworth Building's top and other aeries, and proved to be a major source of revenue during the Depression.[94]

The facade treatment of the Empire State Building was likewise greatly determined by economic factors. The fenestration reflected the internal division of office cells and structural bays. The spacing of columns on the shorter east and west tower facades was even, while on the north and south faces, the second and ninth bays were wider in response to the capacities of steel and the requirements of wind bracing.[95] The windows on the north and south were grouped in pairs or triples in a 2-3-2, 2-2-2, 2-3-2 rhythm, which allowed for flexible subdivision into office suites and also helped to compose the facade. Some 4,000 of the building's more than 6,400 windows were in the tower. The architects' challenge was to avoid monotony:

> What treatment of these myriad openings in this vast expanse of wall would best retain and express solidity of mass, avoid giving the impression of a perforated shell, add dignity to utility, and through all escape the inherently monotonous gridiron of oft-repeated floors crossed by the slotted vertical bands of uniformly spaced windows?[96]

Their solution was to eliminate typically deep (four- to eight-inch) window reveals, by placing the glass on the face of the wall. The limestone panels were simplified and standardized, and all exterior masonry was carried directly on the spandrel beams, omitting shelf angles and brackets. Chrome and nickel steel mullions ran the height of the shaft, both emphasizing the verticals and allowing for the windows and aluminum spandrels to be installed with little exterior scaffolding. The brick enclosing walls were thus constructed from the interior in any convenient order. *(Figs. 98, 99)* These innovations greatly increased speed and economy. As Shreve noted: "The simplicity of the structure and its freedom from numerous small and relatively complicated members aided in making possible the most rapid delivery and erection of steel tonnage in the history of New York."[97]

The factor of time was of key importance. During the construction phase, in addition to the costs of building, developers incur carrying charges which include items such as the interest on the mortgage, taxes, etc.; thus the imperative for speed discouraged any complicated engineering or special orders that would slow the design or building process.[98] The proverbial "time is money" was even more important in the 1920s, when business-space leases were signed annually on the first of May. Unless construction was scheduled so that the space would be ready for May occupancy, rental income would be sacrificed for an entire year, while an empty building continued to run up fixed costs.[99] Indeed, as William Lamb noted, the factor of time was written into the architects' program for the Empire State Building: the completion date was only eighteen months from the beginning of the sketches.

In responding to specific conditions of site, budget, program, and schedule, every skyscraper poses a somewhat different economic and design problem. The complex equation of the Empire State was perhaps best stated in a 1930 article in *Fortune*:

> These various elements fixed the perimeter of an oddly shaped geometric solid, bounded on one side by 83,860 square feet of land, on the other by $35,000,000, on the other by the law of diminishing returns, on another by the laws of physics and the characteristics of structural steel, and on another by the conical exigencies of the zoning ordinances, and on still another by May 1, 1931.[100]

Breaking the Mold

Though each highrise solution is in some sense unique, New York buildings of the 1920s clearly represented a distinctive formal type: the setback skyscraper. The similarities were essential, the differences superficial. Owners and architects, of course, endeavored to distinguish their buildings from others. Individualization was generally achieved on the facade through the choice of materials, fenestration pattern, and ornament. Exterior cladding included limestone, brick, terra-cotta, metal, and, after a revision of the building code in 1937, glass.[101] The choice was a matter of budget, with limestone being the most costly material. Windows were usually evenly spaced or paired, but could be composed with patterns of texture, color, or ornament. In the twenties, verticals were often emphasized, whereas in the late 1940s and 1950s, many setbacks featured horizontal bands of white glazed-brick spandrels and ribbon windows in the Corbusian manner of *fenêtres en longeur.*

The logic of the setback solution was so strong that few architects made an effort to manipulate the formula. One who did was Raymond Hood. Disliking the pyramidal setback, he managed to turn several of his commissions into the form that he preferred: the tower.[102] Given the parameters of the zoning envelope, a sheer tower seemed almost impossible in a for-profit building, but Hood possessed a rare combination of architectural intelligence through which he both created an alternative design that was economically sound, and business acumen, by which he managed to sell the concept to the client. He applied this approach in the Daily News Building (1930), where he first convinced his client to build a mixed-use skyscraper with rental space, rather than simply a publishing plant, then persuaded him to erect less office space on the lower floors than zoning would have allowed in order to produce a more dramatic architectural form.[103] Above the ninth floor on the main Forty-second Street facade, the Daily News rose straight up without setbacks (the rear, however stepped up in multiple recessions). The effect of soaring verticality derived both from the lack of recessions and from the bold pattern produced by the piers, which were faced with white glazed brick that alternated with dark

Fig. 100 Daily News Building (1930).

bands of windows and black and beige brick spandrels. *(Fig. 100)* These
stark stripes represented one of the simplest and also most radical exterior
treatments of the decade. Yet, even more innovative in relation to other
buildings of the period was the tower-like form that Hood created within
the zoning envelope.

Another of the few buildings that broke the mold of the ziggurat was
the RCA Building, the seventy-story structure that was the centerpiece of
Rockefeller Center, the commercial complex of office towers, theaters, and
shops that occupied three full blocks between Forty-eighth and Fifty-first
streets and Fifth and Sixth Avenues.[104] *(Figs. 101–103)* Hood was again the
principal designer, working in collaboration with two other firms as The
Associated Architects of Rockefeller Center. The site of the RCA Building
was as large as that of the Empire State—more than two acres—so the

Fig. 101 Midtown Manhattan and Rockefeller Center, 1932.

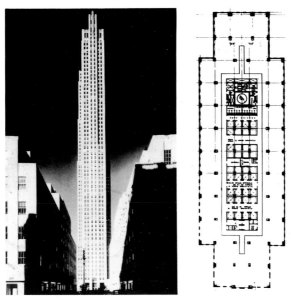

Figs. 102, 103 RCA Building (1932). View from Fifth Avenue, plan.

architects had great latitude to develop the massing within the zoning envelope. Two closely related problems were drawing pedestrians from Fifth Avenue into the interior of the long east-west block and making the building more easily accessible from Sixth Avenue. The solution for these conditions was a long and narrow, essentially rectangular, form that some have referred to as an early example of the "slab."[105] Its base section filled the width of the block, 199 feet, and stretched 465 feet along the crosstown streets; the tower ranged from 70 to 105 feet wide and was 327 feet long. The skyscraper thus presented two contrasting characters depending on one's vantage point. From a distance and from most elevated views, the narrow front and long lateral facades seemed like an expansive wall, while seen from the controlled axis of Fifth Avenue, the slender main facade rose straight up, a soaring tower. *(Figs. 101, 102)*

The slab-like massing of the RCA Building was unusual in New York, but the plan of a typical floor revealed the tower's conformity with market norms. *(Fig. 103)* The elevator banks and other services were grouped in a central core, as in the Chrysler and Empire State Buildings, and were sur-rounded by a full perimeter of offices. These suites were twenty-seven feet deep from window to corridor wall, which, as Hood explained, "experi-ence has proved is the maximum to be allowed to provide adequate light and air to all parts of the building." He further noted how this standard affected the recessions that articulated the lateral facades. As each elevator shaft ended, the building was cut back to maintain the same twenty-seven feet from the core to the exterior walls: "By doing so, we have eliminated every dark corner; there is not a single point in the rentable area of the building that is more than twenty-seven feet away from a window."[106] As in the Empire State Building, the height was decided by calculating the num-ber of elevators required, the cost of materials, and numerous other fac-tors. In an article on the planning of the complex, another of the Rockefeller Center architects, L. Andrew Reinhard, wrote: "What deter-mined the tower height? Figures—cost and return!"[107] Indeed, all of the other design decisions he discussed were similarly determined by econom-ics.

In principle, form follows finance suggests that there is one best solu-tion for a highrise building. What the examples in this section demonstrate is that the multiple variables of the economic equation for every project can produce slightly different solutions. Factors affecting design decisions include the size and location of the lot, the cost of land, average rents for the area, and budget, among many others. The zoning envelope narrowed the options for massing, especially for buildings on small and medium sites, where it left little latitude within the template. For large lots, such as those of the Empire State and RCA Buildings, though, there was considerable freedom within the envelope, and the specific shape of the building was tailored by the logic of economics more than by the limits of the law.

The distinctive formal development of the setback skyscraper pro-duced by the combination of municipal code and market formulas took on the authority of a style by the late 1920s. In *The American Architecture of To-day*, G. H. Edgell called the effects of New York's ordinance "the most interesting single phenomenon in American architecture today." He further noted: "The zoning law taught practicality and suggested design as well. In no other way can the desired effect be got so completely, and the best proof of it is the number of skyscrapers that have been designed in accordance with the scheme in cities in which no such law exists."[108] Detroit, St. Louis, Pittsburgh, and San Francisco, for example, had one or more buildings that adopted a setback-type massing (though, often, the recessions were used only in a decorative manner on the upper floors).[109] Vogue is important in commercial architecture, and New York skyscrapers defined modernity in American culture of the twenties. But if form sometimes follows fashion, it does so only to the extent that it fits comfortably within the budget.

Fig. 104 Aerial view of twenties towers.
Left foreground: Foreman State National Bank Building (1930), One North LaSalle (1930).
Background: Field Building (1934), Board of Trade (1930).

Fig. 105 Skyscrapers along Chicago River and North Michigan Avenue.

Chicago: Twenties Towers

In 1923, Chicago abandoned its cap on building height and passed a zoning law that permitted towers. By 1930, more than twenty spires punctured the old 260-foot limit. The tallest was the 612-foot Board of Trade, but there were also eight buildings higher than 500 feet and eleven exceeding 400 feet. This proliferation of towers was the product of two factors: the real estate boom of the twenties and the passage of the city's first zoning ordinance. *(Figs. 104, 105)*

As in New York, pressure from the real estate market stimulated the new regulations, but in Chicago, the impetus for zoning came from demand rather than from oversupply. The 130-foot height limitation passed in 1893 had been raised and lowered several times in response to real estate cycles and office vacancy rates.[110] The city had enjoyed a pattern of gradual and sustained growth from the turn of the century until World War I, but the military effort stanched development at the same time that businesses were expanding, putting great pressures on existing rents, which increased eighty to one-hundred percent between 1919 and 1924.[111] This situation fueled a boom in construction. New buildings rented quickly and

Figs. 106 Carbide and Carbon Building (1929), shows base-with-tower form.
Fig. 107 One North LaSalle (1930), shows integrated massing and central tower.

were extremely profitable, attracting more investors, and easy financing through banks, insurance companies, and mortgage bond houses excited speculation. Real estate bonds, which were sold to the public like stocks, became a popular form of investment and greatly increased the funds available for new construction. In addition, "shoestring financing" made it possible in many cases to undertake a project with only a small cash downpayment and allowed one-hundred percent mortgage financing based on the future value of the building.[112]

The 1923 zoning ordinance responded to these expansionary pressures by increasing the cubic volume permitted in highrise buildings. In this respect, it had the opposite aim of the New York City law of 1916, which greatly reduced the height and bulk of a building that could be erected on a given site. Although Chicago's guidelines were modeled on New York's, the specific formulas differed substantially. The key change was to allow towers. A revision of the height restrictions in 1920 had raised the maximum height above the sidewalk from 200 to 260 feet, while permitting ornamental (i.e., unoccupied) structures to rise up to 400 feet. The Wrigley Building, Chicago Temple, and London Guaranty and Accident Building (now the Stone Container Building) were designed under this regulation, which also governed the competition program for the Tribune Tower. Under the new code, the vertical limit above the sidewalk was 264 feet. Above that height, a tower could be erected on twenty-five percent of the lot. This upper section could not, however, exceed one-sixth of the maximum cubic area of the main building.[113] This volume restriction limited the height of commercially viable towers; about seventeen to twenty stories was the maximum number of tower floors possible for a quarter-block site of around 160 x 170 feet.[114] Although the 264-foot vertical rise was the highest in any American city with regulations, the limit on volume above that height meant that Chicago towers usually looked stunted, especially compared to those in New York.

During the twenties, two typical massing solutions evolved from Chicago's zoning law. The first was a simple hybrid: a base-with-tower form. This solution often presented awkward proportions of a big blocky bottom surmounted by an undersized top, as in the Carbide and Carbon Building. *(Fig. 106)* The second type, which predominated by the end of the decade, had a more integrated massing, in which the central tower seemed to grow out of its flanking wings, as illustrated by One North LaSalle. *(Fig. 107)*

There was also a persistent popularity of the traditional hollow-square plan, perhaps because it was familiar, but also, because it could be highly profitable. Architects Graham, Anderson, Probst and White reprised the

Fig. 108 Straus Building (1924).

classical cube with an interior court in several large buildings of the twenties. An office block for the Federal Reserve Bank, completed just before the passage of zoning, and its neighbor, the Illinois Merchants Bank, which was erected shortly after the ordinance, were near twins. *(Fig. 4, foreground, left and right)* Both featured temple-front entrances, signaling the presence of a second-floor banking hall that occupied the area of the central court. A similar design by the same firm completed in 1927, the Builders' Building, developed the court as an atrium with four floors of showrooms for the display and sale of construction materials and equipment.[115] *(Fig. 161)*

The Straus Building was one of the first major structures to take advantage of the new zoning provision for towers, although the main

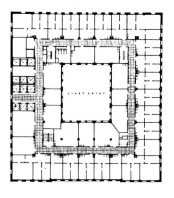

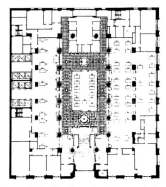

Fig. 109 Straus Building: typical office floor (top), second-floor banking hall (bottom).

body of the building conformed to a typical central court plan. The structure combined a headquarters for the investment banking company S. W. Straus and an income-producing property.[116] A nine-story tower broke through the center eight bays of the twenty-one-story main facade, and was stretched to a height of 475 feet by a solid stepped pyramid and heraldic sculpture. *(Fig. 108)* This tower was a separate section, accessed by its own elevators from the twenty-first floor. Concerned with creating a corporate symbol, the S. W. Straus Company and their architects (again, Graham, Anderson, Probst and White) chose a monumental classical character that they felt communicated strength and stability. A quality image was also important to the speculative aspect of the project, the eighty percent that was marketed to tenants as "Chicago's finest office building." From the outset, the company's Building Committee and the architects collaborated in developing the plans. More than sixty different schemes were considered, and before the design was finalized, it was submitted to a special advisory panel of the National Association of Building Owners and Managers (NABOM). Various suggestions were made and adopted, and the resulting plans were deemed "a development of the site as nearly perfect as it was humanly possible to make it."[117]

The analysis, which was documented in detail, described the economic logic behind nearly every decision of the design. The aim was to achieve the highest ratio of rentable area to the cubic contents of the building and enclosing walls.[118] The plot solution for the large lot (171 feet on Michigan Avenue and 160 feet on Jackson) was a hollow square. *(Fig. 109)* This arrangement produced more square feet of rentable space than a U-shaped plan, and afforded greater flexibility in the placement of elevators and the service core. The committee advised that the spacing of structural columns be seventeen feet, with a depth from windows to corridor of twenty-five to thirty feet. These dimensions fit the ideal "T" layout, which allowed two windowed private offices and a reception area roughly eight feet deep by seventeen feet wide. *(See Fig. 11)* For maximum freedom of planning, outlets were placed on outer columns rather than on partitions, which were built in only after space was leased. Another key decision was the number of elevators, since the quality of service directly affected rents. The standard for a first-class building was a maximum waiting time of twenty-five to thirty seconds during peak periods. By projecting the total population of the building (some 4,000–5,000 tenants and visitors) and the daily traffic pattern, the consultants determined that twelve cars were needed for public use.[119] These were placed on the south side of the property, so as not to preclude the possibility of future expansion, and were arranged in two banks with three cars on each side of the corridor. The separate banks served different zones, which was the first time such a system had been adopted in Chicago.

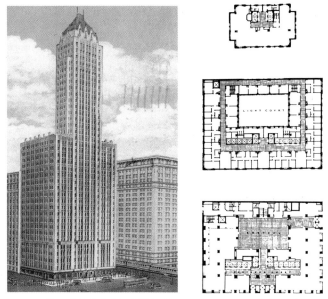

Figs. 110, 111 Pittsfield Building (1922). View and plan.

The money spent creating a quality property was well invested. The value of the building as an advertisement, though difficult to quantify, was certainly of benefit to S. W. Straus, as was the impressive second-floor banking hall. The company reserved four floors of offices for its own purposes, while the remaining floors were leased at some of the highest rates in the city, ranging from $7.00 per square foot in the tower (which was comparable to premium Wall Street prices) to $3.00 for the lower floors of the interior court; the average was about $5.00. The total rentable area of the building comprised 440,000 square feet and the area per floor was 17,068 square feet. The ratio of income-producing space to gross floor area was 74.2 percent; 85 percent of the space was leased within the first year.[120]

In contrast to the Straus Building, where the tower was not integral with base, in the Pittsfield Building, the same architects combined a central-court plan with a tall tower and with elevators that ran from bottom to top. *(Figs. 110, 111)* The standard base rose straight up to the maximum height, in this case twenty-one stories. A slender tower in the center

Figs. 112, 113 Jewelers Building and Roanoke Tower (both 1926).

of the Washington Street facade continued the sheer plane, then stepped
back at the top floors in a series of finials, dormers, and an ornamental
copper roof. Erected by the Marshall Field estate as an investment property, the Pittsfield Building capitalized on its location in the heart of the
retail district at Washington and Wabash with a five-story shopping court.
Like the 1914 Marshall Fields Annex Building across the street by the
same firm, it was marketed as offices for doctors and dentists, a use that
generated considerable numbers of potential shoppers. The light court and
commercial atrium were positioned behind the tower, which allowed the
elevators banks to be brought closer to the entrance.[121] *(Fig. 111)* In this
building, the architects abandoned their customary classicism and
employed a gothic vocabulary that accentuated the verticality of the tower.

Figs. 114, 115 333 North Michigan Avenue and Mather Tower (both 1928).

New Formal Solutions

Despite the financial success of the Straus headquarters and the experiment of the Pittsfield, the hollow-square plan was used infrequently after the passage of zoning. Clearly, an approach that placed all offices on the outside and used the dark center of the building for circulation and utilities had numerous advantages over one that had to enclose an empty light court with expensive windowed walls. But some owners and architects searched for innovative uses for the deep space at the center of large structures. In the Jewelers Building (later, the Pure Oil Building), a 600-car parking garage serviced by elevators extended from the basement level through the twenty-third floor. *(Fig. 112)* The mechanical system, which had frequent failures, was closed in 1940, and the experiment was not repeated elsewhere.[122]

By the mid-1920s, tower schemes with a compact core became the predominant type, both because of the efficiency of the plan and because

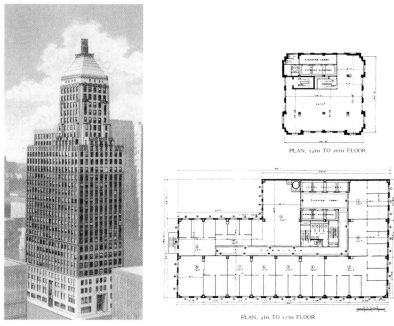

PLAN, 24TH TO 26TH FLOOR

PLAN, 4TH TO 17TH FLOOR

Figs. 116, 117 Trustees System Service Building (1930). View and plans.

the form became associated with modernity. As in New York, the position of the core depended on a variety of factors, including the size of the lot, neighboring structures, and renting strategies. Unlike the hollow-square schemes where elevators were placed in one long line, and stairs, toilets, and other utilities were separated, in the compact-core plan, such facilities were generally grouped together, and elevators were arranged in banks, as in the Trustees System Service Building. *(Figs. 116, 117)*

The most common massing solution was a simple composite of a tall base and a small tower, usually with the tower section pushed toward the major facade to create a more emphatic verticality. The base almost always rose sheer to 264 feet, the maximum height allowed by zoning, and covered the full lot, which was in most cases less than a quarter of a block and therefore rectangular. Because the tower was limited to only one-sixth the volume of the base, the upper section often appeared undersized or truncated, as in the Carbide and Carbon or the Trustees System Service

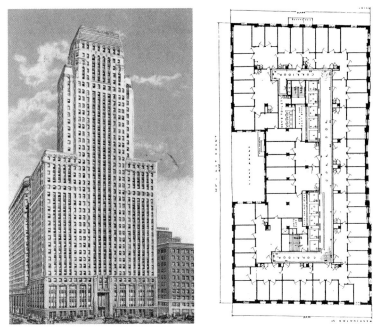

Figs. 118, 119 Foreman State National Bank Building (1930). View and typical floor plan.

Buildings. *(Figs. 106, 116)* Structures on small sites, such as Roanoke Tower, 333 Michigan Avenue or the Mather Tower, had more attenuated proportions, but their tower floors afforded very little rental space. *(Figs. 113–115)*

Larger parcels allowed a more substantial tower. The Foreman State National Bank Building piled thirty-eight stories—sixteen tower floors—on the site of the demolished thirteen-story Chamber of Commerce Building. *(Figs. 118, 49)* The main facade was twice the building's depth, and the tower, which also had flattened proportions, rose flush with the expanse of the limestone-clad base. The plan of the tower floors shows a full perimeter of offices. *(Fig. 119)* A similar massing was employed on a larger scale in the Chicago Civic Opera Building, a mixed-use project that combined two theaters with an office tower that reached forty-two stories. On the east facade, the base and shaft presented a monotonous plane of masonry punched with hundreds of small windows. *(Fig. 120)* On the west, the

119

Fig. 120 Chicago Civic Opera Building (1929).
View from Wacker Drive.

massing and fenestration were more varied and sculptural, indeed, like the second formal type.[123] *(Fig. 121)*

By the late 1920s, a massing solution that better integrated the base and tower sections became popular. This new approach gave the impression of one central tower emerging from a low base (usually four to six stories) and flanked by tall wings of about twenty-three or twenty-four stories, the maximum height allowed by zoning. Examples included One North LaSalle and the LaSalle-Wacker, Bankers, Field, and Board of Trade Buildings. *(Figs. 107, 122–125)* Most of these were forty or more stories. On the lower floors, they were configured in an "H" or "U" plan with a light court that opened onto the major street rather than onto the back alley, as had been typical in the 1890s and early 1900s. Of the two formal approaches, the integrated central tower was generally adopted in buildings that were modernistic in style. The LaSalle-Wacker and Board of Trade

Fig. 121 Chicago Civic Opera Building (1929).
View from Chicago River.

Buildings, in particular, represented the so-called "stripped" style, a moderate modernism that emphasized simplified, hard-edged forms, usually with restrained ornament carved in low relief within the plane of the walls. The decorative treatment on the Field Building, for example, alternated vertical bands of light limestone panels and dark windows and spandrels, somewhat like those of Hood's Daily News Building, though not nearly so bold.[124] *(Figs. 100, 130)*

The forty-five story Board of Trade Building was Chicago's Empire State in both its dominance on the skyline and its efficient office planning. The design was by architects Holabird and Root, who, much like the New York firm of Shreve, Lamb and Harmon, specialized in commercial buildings and were keenly aware of market formulas.[125] The large lot, 173 x 255 feet, had a unique siting that ensured good light and high visibility. Constructed on the site of the nineteenth-century Board of Trade, which

Figs. 122, 123 Bankers Building (1926), LaSalle-Wacker Building (1930).

anchored the financial district *(Fig. 40)*, the skyscraper occupied a full block at the southern end of the Loop where the square grid broke into long rectangles. This block terminated the axis of South LaSalle, and the tight corridor of the office buildings to the north turned the street-level view of the Board of Trade into a dramatic forced perspective. *(Fig. 125)* Visually, these neighboring highrises sliced off the breadth of the twenty-story wings and collapsed their substantial depth, accentuating the building's height. Because of the complex program for the lower floors, which included the trading room and other Board facilities, the office tower was pushed to the southern end of the site. The base section was a deep "U" with the two wings each measuring 120 feet deep by 60 feet wide. *(Fig. 126)* Offices lined a double-loaded corridor and were divided in the familiar "T" layout, with a depth of twenty-seven feet facing streets and twenty-two feet on courts; column spacing permitted an average width of eight or nine feet for offices. *(Fig. 127)* The plans, which were reviewed by the

Figs. 124, 125 Field Building (1934), Board of Trade Building (1930).

Building Planning Service of NABOM, were a model of flexibility and plan efficiency.[126]

A striking contrast to the high-volume, by-the-book plans of the Board of Trade was another building by Holabird and Root that gambled with orthodoxies. The Palmolive Building, a combined corporate headquarters and rental property, was located one mile from the central business district at the northern end of North Michigan Avenue, near the lake and Gold Coast residences. Commercial development on the city's new boulevard had begun in the early 1920s at the southern end, just across the Chicago River from the Loop, with the construction of the Wrigley Building and the plans for the Tribune Tower. Most of the highrises constructed farther to the north in the next years were clubs or hotels.[127] The Palmolive Building was the first tall office building in the area and at thirty-seven stories, towered over its surroundings, enjoying its status as a landmark, as well as superb light and views. *(Fig. 128)*

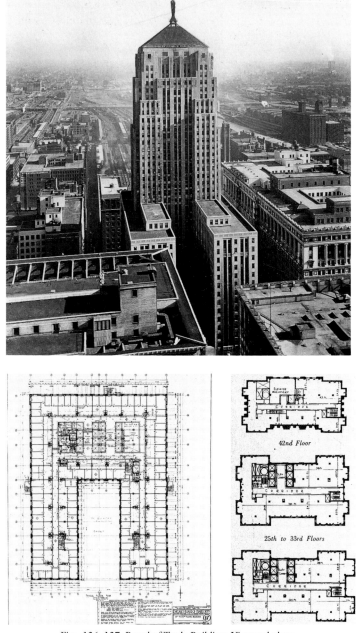

Figs. 126, 127 Board of Trade Building. View and plans.
Note separation of U-shaped base and tower sections.

Erected by the Palmolive-Peet Company, the skyscraper provided the successful soap manufacturer with posh administrative offices as well as a "monument to cleanliness" that enhanced the corporate image.[128] The directors initially planned to construct a lower building, variously reported as five to fifteen stories, which would be the base for a tower to be added at a later date, but after merging with the Colgate Company in 1928, they decided to build the full thirty-seven stories. Only eight floors were used for the corporation's own operations; the remaining floors were to be leased to an elite clientele. The marketing strategy portrayed the distance from the Loop as an asset, emphasizing the lack of traffic congestion and the clean air. "High above the 'dust and fly line' of the city," noted the advertisements, the "executive chambers" in the tower were perfect suites for "estates, capitalists, and retired business men"; general office space was provided in the capacious lower stories.[129] The rental campaign was highly successful; at its opening in May 1929, sixty-five percent of the space was rented to an array of tenants that included many publishers, advertising agencies, and real estate brokers. The street-level and second-floor shops offered convenience and luxury, with a bank, barber shop, beauty parlor, bond brokers, furrier, and other amenities.[130]

The Palmolive Building was unique among Chicago skyscrapers in its New York-style setback massing, a solution influenced by the unusual site and the up-market image. The lot was a substantial parcel, 108 x 231 feet, proportions that were more typical of midtown Manhattan than of the Loop. With an area of about 25,000 square feet, the Palmolive Building covered only about 2,200 square feet less than the Straus Building. The narrow side of the lot was on North Michigan Avenue, so that the building's pyramidal massing was most impressive from that main approach. The facade was richly plastic, with projecting bays alternating with the banding of windows to accentuate the building's height. The setbacks at floors three, eleven, and nineteen were not required by the zoning law, which permitted a sheer vertical rise of 264 feet, but were evidently motivated by aesthetics along with the priority of shallow, well-lit office space (most offices were between eighteen or twenty-six feet deep). The main tower, which began at the twenty-third

Fig. 128 Palmolive Building (1929).

floor, was extremely slender, only 46 x 130 feet; these dimensions consumed the full one-sixth volume allowed for a tower under zoning.[131] After subtracting the area required for elevators and services, the net rentable area per tower floor was only about 4,000 square feet (as compared to the 17,000 square-foot floors of the Straus Building). Within this floor plate, the architects proposed a division into eight offices, ranging in size from 255 to 900 square feet. *(Fig. 129)* Rental brochures extolled the convenience and modernity of the layout: "There is no circling corridor around an inner court to confuse the stranger. One walks straight from the elevators in one direction to any office door."[132] Though relatively small, these suites were richly appointed in a variety of styles from English baronial to modernistic.

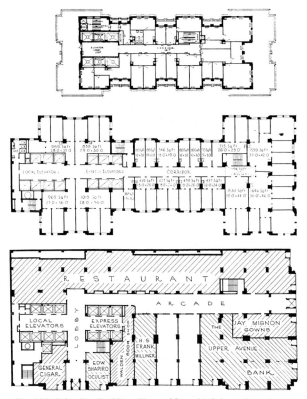

Fig. 129 Palmolive Building. Plans of first, third through tenth, and twenty-second through thirty-second floors.

Historians have described Chicago's tall buildings of the twenties as "setback skyscrapers" modeled on those of Manhattan.[133] But while the Eastern examples clearly influenced the general aesthetic, closer analysis reveals that the typical forms were quite different. The Palmolive Building was the city's only New York-style setback: the characteristic massing solutions in Chicago were the big base-tiny tower hybrid and the integrated base and tower.

Another key difference was height. The footprint of the Palmolive Building was about 4000 square feet larger than that of 500 Fifth Avenue, yet the New York building was twenty-two stories taller. *(Figs. 128 and 84)* No example of stunted growth was more striking than that of the

Fig. 130 Field Building (1934).

Field Building, which occupied the whole southern half of the block between Adams and Monroe and stretched the full distance between LaSalle and Clark Streets.[134] *(Fig. 130)* This site was 160 x 350 feet, about the same area as the main section of the RCA Building and only about one-third smaller than the Empire State. Yet the tower, a simple rectangular slab sandwiched between four tall wings of twenty-two stories, terminated at forty-three stories. Whereas the RCA Building and the Empire State each contained about two million square feet, Chicago's largest office building offered only one million.

Completed in 1934, the Field Building was the final skyscraper of the twenties' boom cycle, which was in a way, poetic, since to construct it, the

Fig. 131 Prudential Building (1955).

Home Insurance Building, the putative first skyscraper, was torn down. No new office space was undertaken in Chicago until 1952, when work began on the Prudential Building. In New York, however, recovery began almost immediately after World War II, and by 1959, 54 million square feet of new office space was completed or in development. In Chicago ,during the same period, only 2.6 million square feet of office space was constructed.[135] The slow growth was attributable to the oversupply of office space from the 1920s, the Depression economy, World War II, and the post-war recovery period. By 1950, though, all the vacant space had been absorbed, and demand was so strong that 2.7 million square feet in loft buildings was converted to office use.[136]

In 1942, when vacancies were still high, the city passed a new ordinance that further reduced the maximum volume of a highrise, this time to 144 feet times the area of the lot (which was about twelve stories if the building covered the full site).[137] To construct thirty or more floors, therefore, the site had to be very large, and most of it would be left empty. The developers of the Prudential Building, which was built over the tracks of the Illinois Central Railroad, had to lease three and a half acres of air rights in order to erect their forty-one story tower. *(Fig. 131)* Under the previous ordinance, the building could have contained more than twice the volume.

In a 1959 study of the relation between height limits and highrise construction in Chicago, Shultz and Simmons argued that the city's zoning law inhibited development, because stringent restrictions on height and volume (at least compared to New York) took the profits out of new construction. Without an attractive rate of return, money found other, more lucrative areas of investment. Corporations that would have preferred to build Chicago headquarters in income-producing structures like the Straus or Palmolive Buildings were discouraged from doing so by the zoning restrictions, and instead moved to other cities, especially to New York.[138] Shultz and Simmons's theory cannot be tested, but the data are consistent with such an explanation. *(See Fig. 162, Part II)* In any case, the most significant fact about the Chicago skyscraper in the post-war decade was its absence.

The interrelated influences of economic height, zoning, and speculative construction and how they affect the morphology of the central business district are further explored in Part II, which takes up the issue of urbanism. The focus here has been on defining the different formal types that evolved in New York and Chicago in response to local conditions and real estate economics. Perhaps because individual buildings present such apparent variety within the types, these distinct vernaculars of capitalism have not been identified as such before this study.

The contrasting forms of the Manhattan tower with a compact core and the Chicago cube with an interior court, or the less dramatic distinctions between twenties towers produced in response to zoning, composed the characteristic skylines of the two cities. *(See Figs. 1–4)* In one sense, skylines are simply the aggregate of typical buildings. But there are other issues beyond the formal that must be considered in order to understand the morphology of skyscraper cities. The spatial and temporal dimensions of skylines, which are likewise affected by municipal regulations and real estate cycles, are manifest in the heights of buildings and density of central business districts. Before turning to these issues, however, several distinctions should be drawn between the vernacular period just surveyed and the international phase of skyscraper design and urbanism of the second half of the century.

Fig. 132 Office interior, Equitable Building, New York (1961).

Postscript: The International Period

In the 1950s, advances in technology and changes in architectural ideology liberated the tall office building from its dependence on nature and site. Fluorescent lighting and air conditioning were as important to the transformation of post-World War II skyscrapers as were the elevator and steel-cage construction to the first tall office buildings of the late nineteenth century. Produced at an affordable price from the late thirties, fluorescent bulbs provided high levels of illumination without excessive heat, making it possible to rent quality office space much deeper than the old standard of twenty-eight to thirty feet. Cool fluorescents rendered light courts unnecessary, so that all

internal space could be exploited. Although open work areas were hardly new *(See "Metropolitan Belles" in Fig. 12)*, the modernist concept of the open plan, in which expansive space was an aesthetic in itself, was facilitated by the new technology. *(Fig. 132)* The model office became the clean, well-lighted place; in the 1930s, the standard level of illumination was still only 25 foot-candles, but by the 1960s, 100 footcandles was common.[139] In many postwar buildings, the ceiling became a gridded plane of light in which accoustical material and ventilating equipment were also concealed. Since large windows were no longer necessary to illuminate interiors, ceiling heights could be reduced, and more stories could be fit within the zoning envelope.

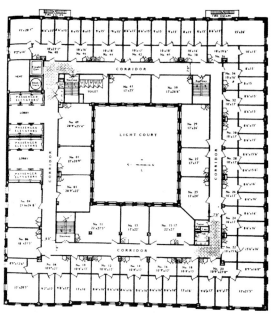

Fig. 133 Straus Building (1924).
plans are shown at the same scale

The most visually striking change in postwar skyscrapers was the glass facade. Glass was transfomed—from window panes to curtain walls—more for fashion than for function. In 1955, Shultz and Simmons noted that glass walls had "no financial purpose, except as advertising," but had numerous drawbacks, including sun glare, inceased costs of heating and cooling, and the installation of blinds or drapes.[140] As operable windows became outmoded, interiors of necessity were artifically climate controlled.

The growing influence of the International Style and the concept of the tower in the plaza also broke down the traditional connection of the building to the boundaries of its lot. Following models such as Lever House *(Fig. 136)* and the Seagram Building in New York or Inland Steel, Federal Center, and the Equitable Building in Chicago, by the mid-1960s, the pristine glass box became the dominant form for the modern sky-scraper. In prestige commissions of this type, the building was often placed in a plaza and presented as a discrete object in space, rather than as a part of the urban fabric. *(Figs. 137, 138)* Ironically though, as technology freed

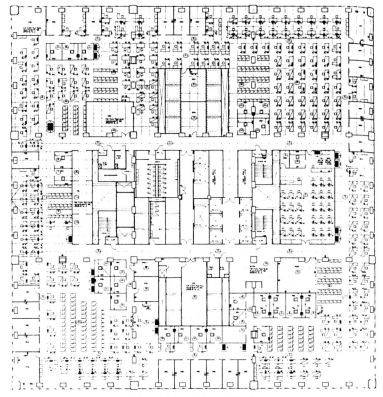

Fig. 134 Sears Tower (1974).
plans are shown at the same scale

tall buildings to take any form, the orthodoxy of high modernism tended to standardize them.

The shifts in formal type from the typical New York setback and the Chicago base-plus-tower approaches also had a programmatic basis in changing needs for space and layout within offices. Businesses had prospered during the war years and needed additional space for their expanding workforce and new types of equipment. From 1940 to 1960, employment of white-collar workers doubled, as did the area of the average office. In 1965, the average tenant occupied 2,622 square feet, double the area of 1952, which was the first year such a figure was reported.[141] Many companies preferred to consolidate operations on large, full floors and utilized

Figs. 135, 136 100 Park Avenue (1949), Lever House (1952).

space far from windows for clerical staff, meeting rooms, and office machines. Describing the advantages of the new buildings over those of the twenties, Lee Thompson Smith, president of the Real Estate Board of New York, wrote in 1950:

> These buildings are modern. Primarily because they are air conditioned. But one salient characteristic of the new buildings that cannot be adapted to old buildings at any price is their basic planning. They provide large blocks of space on one floor, with great glass areas, better lighting, fewer courts, less waste space, and new automatic elevator arrangements, with fewer cars and faster service. Deeper floor areas, among the other developments in design, result in as much as eighty percent of the space on each floor being rentable space, as compared with sixty-five percent in the buildings that were conventional twenty years ago.[142]

Figs. 137, 138 First National City Bank (399 Park Avenue) (1959),
One Chase Manhattan Plaza (1960).

Smith was referring to New York buildings of the 1950s such as 100 Park Avenue, which was the first major office building constructed in the Grand Central district since the early thirties. *(Fig. 135)* Finished in 1949, the thirty-six story structure occupied the full width of the block (200 feet) with 240 feet of frontage on Fortieth Street and 146 feet on Forty-first Street. The large plot allowed individual floors of 32,000 square feet on the base stories, and around 14,500 to 9,500 square feet for tower floors.[143] The building was fully air-conditioned, and all interior spaces, even areas fifty or sixty feet from a window, were usable. One of the first examples of a common solution for major New York highrises of the fifties, 100 Park Avenue was a perfect example of what the industry called "block type buildings," structures with floorplates that could accommodate tenants requiring 25,000 square feet or more.[144] Still governed by the setback formula, these buildings generally had bulky base sections uncut by light

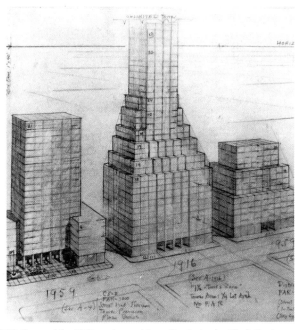

Fig. 139 Proposal for 1961 zoning revisions. Rendering by Hugh Ferriss contrasts
1916 setback formula with FAR formula in tower and plaza design.

courts, several setbacks of two or three stories each, and an abbreviated
tower of ten to fifteen stories. Few buildings of this period were particularly tall: of the 109 buildings erected in Manhattan from 1947 to 1960, only
20 were thirty or more stories, of which 5 exceeded forty stories.[145] Despite
their relatively stubby proportions, these buildings were very profitable; the
Real Estate Board of New York calculated that these highrises provided an
average of three-fifths more rentable floor space than structures erected
between 1925 and 1933.[146]

In Chicago during the same period, new office buildings saw the same
sixty percent increase in volume over those of the twenties. As a result of a
1955 revision of the zoning ordinance that raised the floor area ratio
(FAR) to sixteen (i.e., sixteen times the area of the lot) from a formula that
had imposed an FAR of approximately twelve, the average rentable area of
new structures of the 1960s grew substantially, from around 200,000 in

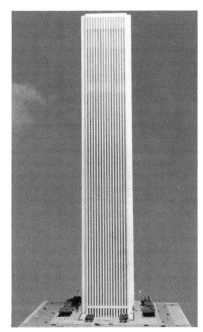

Figs. 140, 141 General Motors Building, New York (1968),
Standard Oil Building (now Amoco), Chicago (1974).

the 1950s to about 317,000 from 1960 to 1965.[147] This rose even more
dramatically in the later sixties and early seventies, when the skyline added
several giants, including the Standard Oil (now Amoco; *Fig. 141*) and John
Hancock Buildings, which were both over 1,100 feet high, and the 1974
Sears Tower, which at 110 stories and 1,450 feet became the world's
tallest building. A comparison of typical floor plans of the Sears Tower and
the 1924 Straus Building illustrates the striking increase in rentable area
that could be achieved from fluorescent lights and air conditioning. *(Figs.
133, 134)* The exterior walls of the Straus's hollow-square structure
enclosed 27,360 square feet, but due to the light court, the rentable area
was only 17,068 square feet. In the Sears Tower, where the elevators and
mechanical systems were located in a central core and all interior space was
utilized, the area of the largest floors was around 50,000 square feet, or
about fifty percent larger than the Straus Building; about 40,000 square

Fig. 142 Sears Tower, Chicago (1974).

feet of these floors was rentable, more than twice the usable area in the Straus plan. In the Sears plan, areas as deep as seventy feet were used as workspace.[148]

In New York, the first finite limits on volume (and therefore on height) were imposed in 1961, when the 1916 zoning ordinance received its first major revision. The chief motivation for the 1961 zoning resolution was to reduce the bulk of buildings and, by extension, the overall density of the future city.[149] Like Chicago, it did so by establishing an FAR formula, eliminating the open-ended provision for unrestricted height over one quarter of the lot. *(Fig. 139)* A simple idea with a handbook of variations, FAR keyed the amount of floor space permitted in a building to the area of its lot.[150] The highest basic FAR in office districts was fifteen. This could be increased twenty percent to an FAR of eighteen, if a developer included a public plaza or arcade. Such "incentive zoning" was designed to

Fig. 143 Chicago skyline.

create more open space at street level in the city's most dense districts. The new ordinance encouraged tower-in-the-plaza schemes by increasing the area of coverage of towers from the twenty-five percent to forty percent of the lot.[151] Thus the FAR formula effectively ended the standard setback massing, not because the new code prohibited it, but because sheer-walled towers in open plazas became more profitable.

This study has emphasized that skyscraper design takes place within tight parameters of program and economics which make formal invention unusual. Yet, taste clearly matters. The paradigmatic International Style skyscrapers of the 1950s, such as Lever House, the Seagram Building, and One Chase Manhattan Plaza, exerted a major influence on contemporaries. Erected by powerful corporations seeking to project an image of affluence and modernity, these elegant monoliths indulged in the luxury of empty space. The towers were set back from sidewalks in private plazas,

Fig. 144 World Trade Center and Battery Park City skyline.

eschewing lucrative street-level commercial rents. Other buildings, such as the Park Avenue headquarters of Union Carbide and First National City Bank *(Fig. 136)*, emulated the tower-and-plaza model even before the change in the zoning law. But the popularization of the type came after 1961, when the aesthetic values it represented were written into the zoning law. One reason skyscrapers in New York, Chicago, and elsewhere looked so much alike from the 1950s through the 1970s was due to the hegemony of the Modern Movement in the American architectural profession.

By the late 1970s, the orthodoxy of the International Style began to break down under the new aesthetics and ideology of postmodernism. At the same time, computer technology created a demand for a new office plan. Many companies preferred large open floors of 20,000 to 30,000 square feet in "smart buildings" wired for advanced electronic systems. A favored office floor plan called for a consistent dimension of between thirty-five to forty-five feet from the core to the enclosing outside wall. Architect William Pedersen of Kohn, Pedersen and Fox, one of the most successful firms of the eighties, noted: "The ideal building, from the functional point of view, calls for a square plan with each of its sides...approximately 145 to 175 feet."[152] Such structures tended to look somewhat stubby or swollen, rather than sleek and soaring. Examples include the World Financial Center at Battery Park City *(Fig. 144)* and Worldwide Plaza in New York, and the AT&T Corporate Center and Leo Burnett Building in Chicago. These buildings ranged from thirty-four to sixty stories, heights typical for such jumbo schemes. Facade treatments often alluded to historical styles and revived the use of traditional materials such as stone or brick (applied in thin prefabricated panels), yet the variety of ornamental motifs designed to differentiate these buildings mark them all as postmodern. *(Fig. 143)*

A chart of the tallest office buildings over the past hundred years would show an impressive ascent from Chicago's Masonic Temple to the Sears Tower, or from New York's Woolworth and Empire State Buildings to the twin towers of the World Trade Center. Yet, the history of the skyscraper has not been a steady progress from small to tall. Nor has great height been motivated simply by advances in technology and the urges of advertising or ego. Land-use regulation and real estate economics have affected building height and form as much as have engineers and architects. Skyscrapers are shaped by program, profit, technology, taste, and, especially during the vernacular period, by nature and place.

Fig. 145 Aerial view of Manhattan.

Part II

Just Speculating: Observations on the Dynamics of CBDs

The common cliche "the corporate skyline" suggests that American cities have been dominated by structures built by and symbolic of "Big Business." The phrase offers an easy shorthand for the increasing influence of corporations in the country's economy and culture, but it is profoundly misleading as a description of the dynamics of downtown growth. In all periods, the majority of skyscrapers have been speculative, not corporate buildings. Central business districts, or CBDs, must be understood as complex, competitive commercial markets where space is a commodity, and location and image count.

From the 1880s through the 1920s, the consolidation and restructuring of industry and business and the rise of managerial, or corporate capitalism helped transform American cities and culture. Social and urban historians have analyzed how production and administration became separated, with executives and office workers located in urban buildings near financial and other services.[1] The increasing wealth and power of the corporate sector and the rapid expansion of the white-collar workforce, including large numbers of women, gave rise to looming office buildings and lavish headquarters. In histories of the skyscraper, such conspicuous spires as the Singer, Metropolitan Life, and Woolworth Buildings have become standard representations of the growing presence and power of corporations in the modern city.

Indeed, scholars in various disciplines have equated big business and big buildings. Characterizing the different values of nineteenth- and twentieth-century city builders, cultural historians Thomas Bender and William Taylor contrasted the "civic horizontalism" of the earlier period with the "corporate verticality" of the modern metropolis.[2] "Vertical expressions of corporate power" was the phrase used by social historian Olivier Zunz to describe early-twentieth-century skylines.[3] Many architectural historians have explained skyscrapers as expensive expressions of corporate identity or as advertising. Kenneth Gibbs stated the central concern of his study of skyscrapers from the 1870s through the 1930s to be "the manner in which the tall office building functioned as an image-forming vehicle for big business."[4] William Jordy referred to highrise development such as Rockefeller Center as "corporate urbanism."[5]

The words *skyscrapers* and *corporate buildings* are used interchangeably by many authors. For some, the association seems simply an elision—that is, they fail to mention any buildings erected as rental properties.[6] For others it reflects ideological assumptions. Marxist social scientists Joe Feagin and Robert Parker explain the growth of skylines in the first three decades of the twentieth century as paralleling the expansion of large independent and merged corporations during the "rise of oligopoly capitalism"; such firms, they claim, "sought larger buildings for their functional utility and for their symbolism of power."[7] While not false, such statements imply that most skyscrapers have been built, owned, or are occupied principally by large companies—which is demonstrably untrue.

Speculative buildings—structures erected by individuals or groups of investors purely as rental properties—have greatly outnumbered corporate construction in every period of skyscraper history. Most corporate headquarters also lease a major portion of their building to outside tenants. This chapter argues that all skyscrapers—even corporate showcases—can be viewed as real estate ventures, either as income-generating properties or as long-term investments in high-value urban land.

Few architectural historians have considered speculative skyscrapers either as a type or as forces shaping the skyline. The best work on the

Figs. 146, 147 Singer Building (1908) and Woolworth Building (1913) in context.

subject is an article by Gail Fenske and geographer Deryck Holdsworth, which despite its title, "Corporate Identity and the New York Office Building, 1895–1915," addresses both corporate and speculative buildings. Fenske and Holdsworth identify two forces as "agents of New York's transformation from a mid-nineteenth-century city, with an extended village-like character, to a twentieth-century skyscraper city."[8] One was the "large-scale commercial enterprises, whose presence was announced by larger and larger business buildings identified with company names." The other was "scores of smaller commercial and professional firms...and their demand for office space close to key sites and key enterprises."[9] In addition to the familiar topic of "Who built skyscrapers?" the authors thus posed a more original and intriguing question: "Who occupied them?"

Their research revealed that, in most cases, the occupants were not exclusively the companies that erected the trademark towers. In the forty-seven-story Singer Building on lower Broadway, *(Fig. 146)* the company's

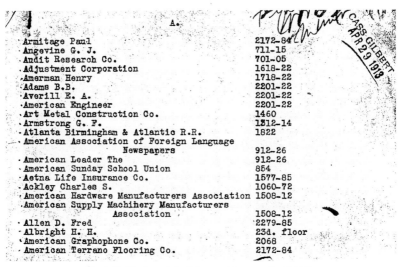

Fig. 148 Woolworth Building partial tenant list (1913).

offices occupied just one floor of the tower; all others were rented, mostly to lawyers and financial services. Of the fifty-five stories of the Woolworth Building, that company's operations filled less than two floors, while the remaining space was leased, generally as small offices. *(Figs. 147, 148)* A list of tenants in 1913 recorded around 600 names of individuals or companies; another of 1924 listed more than 400 lessees, including such enterprises as the Nestlé Food Company, the Honolulu Iron Works, American Linseed Company, Patent Vulcanite Roofing, Bridgeport Brass, and the Franco-American Promoting Company. In the base section of the building, from the second through the twenty-fifth floor, there were eighty-five office units per floor, and the majority of tenants rented one to three units.[10] Unfortunately, Fenske and Holdsworth do not fully discuss the implications of these numbers that so underscore the importance of smaller enterprises and professional services in the economics of these corporate buildings. And though they also researched the mixed tenancy of several major speculative structures of the period, their analysis maintains the standard separation of corporate and speculative buildings.

Fig. 149 City Hall Park and early skyscrapers on Park Row, c.1900.
Far left: American Tract Society Building (1894). Middle right: 15 Park Row (1898).

Corporate versus speculative is a false distinction, but, like most old saws, it has some validity. Corporate headquarters are usually treated as an elite group, and because creating identity is part of the function of a head-quarters, many have impressive facades, opulent lobbies, and posh execu-tive offices and board rooms. Because the sole purpose of speculative struc-tures is to make money, budgets and buildings are often spare. Yet almost all corporate-owned buildings rent some of their floors to tenants. Seldom was a headquarters used entirely by a company's own employees, especially in the high-rent central business district. (Buildings such as New York's Lever House [*Fig. 136*] or Chicago's Inland Steel were near anomalies.) Creating a distinctive image is as important for speculative developers as for corporate owners, and they use precisely the same strategies to do so, including height, prime locations, and rich materials. Indeed, the terms used by the real estate industry to describe office buildings refer not to ownership, but to quality: "Class A," "Class B," etc. There is little differ-ence in the interiors of the typical office floors of corporate or speculative buildings; because most corporate buildings were conceived from the outset as revenue-generating properties, the office floor plans had to follow market formulas and be generic and flexible.

In writings on skyscrapers it is considered a verity that companies justified very tall or lavish headquarters as advertising and that a kind of "edifice complex" drove up building heights of corporate towers. Indeed, the most conspicuous presences on the New York skyline in the early twentieth century were the brand-name Singer, Metropolitan Life, and Woolworth Buildings; from 1908 to 1913 each successively took the title of world's tallest building. At other times, though, the loftiest towers were speculative. In 1892 in Chicago, the highest landmark in the Loop was the Masonic Temple, which was financed by stock subscription.[11] In 1898, the tallest structure in Manhattan was the thirty-two story 15 Park Row, erected by a group of investors, the Ivins Syndicate. *(Fig. 149)* Likewise, in the early 1930s, the highest spires of New York—the Empire State, Chrysler, Cities Service, RCA, and Bank of Manhattan Company Buildings—despite some corporate-sounding names, were all speculative ventures. *(Figs. 93, 87, 72, 102, 81)* Extreme height has publicity value that equally benefits corporate or speculative owners.

Far more important than advertising value in driving up building heights were strong demand for office space and costly sites in prime locations. As land prices escalated, taller buildings were required to lower the costs of producing a square foot of rental space. High rents virtually ensured that a corporate building owner in a prestige district would become a landlord. A good example was the Bankers Trust Building at 14 Wall Street, across the street from the New York Stock Exchange. In 1910, the bank had paid the highest price yet recorded for Manhattan land, $820 per square foot, and after demolishing the eighteen-story Gillender Building and adding an adjacent parcel, a thirty-nine story tower was shoehorned onto a site just 90 x 90 feet. *(Figs. 150, 151)* The bank occupied only the lower three floors, renting the stories above, generally as small offices, to law firms, brokers, and other professionals who paid high rates for such a prime location.[12] Bankers Trust's own staff operations were housed in less expensive space elsewhere. Many other examples of using

Figs. 150, 151 Gillender Building (1897) and Bankers Trust (1912).
Successive towers on same site.

tenants to finance a flagship building could be cited; at least forty percent of the floors leased to outside tenants seemed to have been standard through the century. In 1960, when The Chase Manhattan Bank erected its sixty-story headquarters in Lower Manhattan, only the lower half of the building was used by the bank, while floors thirty-four and up (except the top one) were leased.[13] *(Fig. 138)* The rentable area of One Chase Manhattan Plaza is 1,820,000 square feet. In 1995, Chase continued to lease thirty-eight floors of its main building, even though the net office space occupied by corporate operations in buildings in Lower Manhattan exceeded the total area of its headquarters.[14]

Corporations relocating home offices outside prime districts generally constructed more space than they needed, building to the optimal economic formula rather than to their present needs. A good illustration of this was the succession of structures erected by the Metropolitan Life Insurance Company. In the late 1880s, the company sold its building in

151

Fig. 152 Metropolitan Life Insurance Company Headquarters (1893)
with 1909 tower, on Madison Square. Flatiron Building at right.

Lower Manhattan and moved uptown to Madison Square and Twenty-
third Street, where they erected an eleven-story building, completed in
1893. The rapid growth of the business required more and more space for
burgeoning staff and files, and over the next decade, annexes were added
until the headquarters covered nearly the entire block. After acquiring the
last remaining parcel and demolishing the Madison Square Presbyterian
Church, the company erected its fifty-story campanile. On completion in
1909, it was the world's tallest office building, and Metropolitan Life was
the world's largest insurer. Yet throughout these expansions, the company
continued to lease about forty percent of its building to tenants. One function of the record-breaking tower was to proclaim the company's status,
but the income-generating aspects were by no means incidental. In a
report to his board, Vice President Haley Fiske called the tower "a proper
investment of the company's funds" and boasted that it "didn't cost the
company a cent because the tenants footed the bill."[15] *(Fig. 152)*

In addition to the advertising value and additional income from tenants, there were numerous advantages in a company owning its building. Control over the quality of the space, other tenants, and, especially, the duration of occupancy (with no leases to negotiate) proved advantageous for long-range planning. Further, corporate skyscrapers represented valuable assets in urban real estate. Many companies replaced a lowrise structure with a taller one or sold an old building at a profit when they moved or downsized. Some recent examples of "recycling" headquarters in New York include the RCA Building (now GE) at Rockefeller Center, the Pan Am Building (now Met Life), and the AT&T Building (now Sony). *(Figs. 153, 154)* Chicago's most notorious renaming was the *Playboy* headquarters (alias the Palmolive Building). Skyscrapers adapt easily to new uses or owners. In contrast, many suburban "corporate campuses" built in the 1970s and 1980s whose companies have suffered hard times, have become giant white elephants. *(Fig. 155)*

In their article, Fenske and Holdsworth asserted that for advertising value, corporate towers were sited to maximize their "visibility to urban crowds."[16] But while visibility is important, rentability was surely a far more powerful impetus. Unobstructed towers in prime areas offered well-lit office space and views that translated into high rents. Rather than interpreting corporate skyscrapers simply as *representations* of big business, we need to understand them also as *businesses themselves*. Both corporate and speculative buildings are part of a marketplace where the space is for sale, and location and image have value.

The chief consumers in this market were not large corporations, but small and medium-sized companies and firms. The preponderance of small tenants was more pronounced in the first half of the century, but even today, they represent the majority of renters. Around 1900, buildings were usually constructed with individual suites, mostly quite small. One expert noted that offices measuring 10 x 12 feet and 15 x 20 feet (120 to 300 square feet) rented more easily than larger ones.[17] One of the most successful New York highrises of the period was the twenty-story American Tract Society Building, which was divided into more than 700 offices, with thirty-

Figs. 153, 154 Pan Am/Met Life Building.
Corporate buildings are easily recycled.

six per floor, ranging in size from about 100 to 150 square feet.[18] *(Fig. 150)* The Park Row Building contained about 950 offices and some 3,500 tenants.[19] In Chicago, offices were slightly larger, usually around 200 to 300 square feet, but each floor was still divided into many small units.[20] The Masonic Temple had about 600 offices; the Monadnock 1,600.[21] *(plans, Figs. 48, 51)*

Throughout the century, the size of the average office increased, but the proportion of small renters to larger ones remained high. A survey of Detroit buildings in the 1920s showed that eighty-eight percent of downtown tenants occupied less than 1,000 square feet. With an average at that time of about 100 square feet per employee, this meant an office of ten or fewer. Less than two percent of tenants used 6,000 square feet or more.[22] Similarly, in Boston, eighty-seven percent of tenants leased less than 1,000 square feet, while only one percent used more than 4,000 square feet.[23] Even in 1990, according to a recent survey of Chicago buildings, nearly two-thirds of downtown tenants leased spaces of 1,000 to 2,500 square feet.[24]

Looking inside the skyscraper at tenancy, we see not the hive of a single company, but a cross-section of interdependent enterprises and com-

I.B.M. Vacancies Add to Westchester Glut

By MARY VIZARD

A RECENT announcement by I.B.M. that it would vacate 845,000 square feet of office space in two Westchester County buildings has sent the already beleaguered office market in the county reeling.

For one thing, it caused this year's first-quarter office vacancy rate to shoot up 4 points, to 26.4 percent, from three months ago, according to Rostenberg Doern, a Stamford, Conn., brokerage firm that specializes in commercial real estate.

The hardest hit area is downtown White Plains, with a record vacancy rate of 35.8 percent, up from 28.9 percent at the end of last year, according to Rostenberg Doern.

This was caused, in large part, by I.B.M.'s decision to vacate 373,000 square feet in Westchester One, the largest building in White Plains, where the company leases 820,540 square feet. And the company is likely to continue reducing its office space, according to an I.B.M. spokesman, Ken Sayers.

"Our strategy is to gradually move out of leased space as contracts expire and into I.B.M.-owned space," Mr. Sayers said. "Regrettably, the company finds it also needs less company-owned space."

As a result, I.B.M. has placed one of its premiere properties on the market: The 472,639-square-foot, I. M. Pei-designed building at 2000 Purchase Street. Employees will

Fig. 155 Suburban corporate campuses can become white elephants.

peting firms. Many historians view the modern city as being produced by hegemonic forces: large corporations, moneyed interests, and government, usually seen as acting in collusion. Certainly, these are influential, but more significant for explaining CBD growth is the dynamic of small-scale capitalism—that is, both the myriad tenants that fill downtown highrises and the highly diffused and competitive real estate industry that constructs and operates them.

To understand the modern city, it is speculative development we should study. Cities grow primarily in the fits and starts that are real estate cycles. Their skylines—the heights of buildings, their density, and their spatial distribution—graph these cycles in 3-D. For example, the tallest buildings generally appear just before the end of a boom, their height driven up by the speculative fever that affects both developers and lenders. Speculative buildings constitute the majority of structures in every central business district, and they represent about two-thirds to three-quarters of new construction in nearly every period. Historians have paid little attention to this important subject, either as a category of buildings or as individual structures, except when they are the designs of well known architects.

Since there were no industry surveys until the mid-1940s, gauging the degree to which speculative buildings dominated skyscraper construction is difficult for the early decades of the century. My own rough estimate indicated that during the 1920s, when Chicago added some twenty major towers, about a third carried the names of corporations. During the same years in New York, about one hundred major buildings were constructed and the ratio was about four to one. Even in the post-World War II decade, the years most closely associated with corporate expansion and signature headquarters, the preponderance of highrise construction in New York was speculative (also called "competitive"). According to the Real Estate Board of New York, seventy-eight percent of new office construction from 1947 to 1961 was in competitive buildings.[25] In postwar Chicago the stringent zoning discouraged speculative projects for about ten years, but after a change in zoning under Mayor Daley, larger structures were encouraged and building resumed.[26]

Speculative developers represented a wide range of individuals and groups. Some were wealthy figures who regarded commercial architecture as a lucrative area of investment; for example, Peter and Shepherd Brooks, who erected and owned a number of Chicago's early skyscrapers, including the Montauk and Monadnock Buildings, directed their interests from Boston through correspondence with their local agent, Owen Aldis. At the other end of the spectrum were rags-to-riches entrepreneurs such as Fred French and Irwin Chanin, who built up empires by leveraging each building into the next bigger one. Syndicates of stock holders or development corporations, often organized for a single project, were a common way to finance a structure. Some development groups represented two or three major investors, as in New York's Equitable or Empire State Buildings; others represented pooled resources, such as the fraternal orders that erected Chicago's Masonic Temple. Some developers were rich and powerful, others were lean and hungry: all were looking for an attractive return on their investment.

The word *speculative* needs to be examined briefly, since it is often used perjoratively, implying either a tight budget and low quality, or a sort of amoral rapaciousness, as in "greedy speculators." The term, however, simply refers to structures erected as rent-producing properties. Quite literally, developers speculate on the future value of the property, estimating an income stream over the life of the building. Two types of speculative development should be distinguished, which I will call *standard conditions* and *boom behavior*. The former is most important for the general urban scene, while the latter produces the most spectacular buildings.

In normal times, when costs of land, materials, and construction are predictable, developers use well-tested formulas to estimate the economics of a project. These calculations are based on the concept of the capitalization of net income. As Richard Hurd explained in his classic treatise of 1903, *Principles of City Land Values*, capitalization of ground rents (the process of translating future rents into a present value) is the fundamental basis of urban land values.[27] Figuring capitalization involves many factors and multiple steps; from the gross rent of land and building must be deducted all charges for services, taxes, insurance, repairs, depreciations, and interest on the money invested.[28] All these factors are considered over time. The real economic value of property (the price a developer should pay for it or sell it for) therefore becomes, as another expert explained, "the sum of all the net land incomes that will accrue in perpetuity, discounted for the period of time that will elapse before they are received."[29] This value takes into account the net income for thirty or forty years.[30] As discussed in Part I, the conventional market formulas and the concept of economic height were widely known and followed in the industry. Most speculative building was not risky, but reserved in its calculations and highly responsive to market desires.

In booms, the so-called rational basis of land values is disregarded, and the answer to the question "What is the value of land?" becomes "Whatever someone is willing to pay." Some speculators estimate value on new assumptions of higher rents; others simply plan to turn a property for a quick profit. In the rapid population growth and the physical expansion

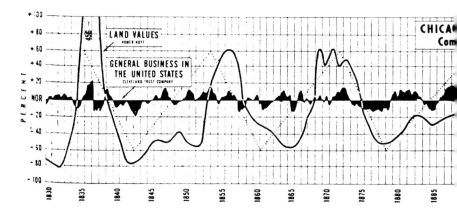

Fig. 156 Homer Hoyt's graph of Chicago land value cycles, 1830 to 1956.

of cities of the late-nineteenth and early-twentieth century, increasing demand for buildings would seem a certainty. But due to the cyclical character of the real estate industry, the timing of a project is crucial to its success, and the amount a property reaps in rents or sale depends on when in a cycle it is completed or comes onto the market.

Empirically, the recurrence of major booms every couple decades has long been noted, but the historical pattern of real estate cycles and a theory of their stages was first formulated in the 1930s in the work of economists such as Homer Hoyt and Roy Wenzlick. In *One Hundred Years of Land Values in Chicago* (1933), Hoyt charted and analyzed the cycles of Chicago real estate from the city's foundation in 1830s.[31] For this extraordinary volume, he poured through tens of thousands of documents, including records of sales, annual reports of conveyances, construction records, and tax assessments, and from these, identified a pattern of demand, development, overbuilding, and decline that recurred five times in the city's hundred-year history. In these cycles he discerned "a series of forces that are to a certain degree independent and yet which communicate impulses to each other in a time sequence, so that when the initial or primary factor appears, it tends to set the others in motion in a definite order."[32] The description of the full cycle was very detailed, with some

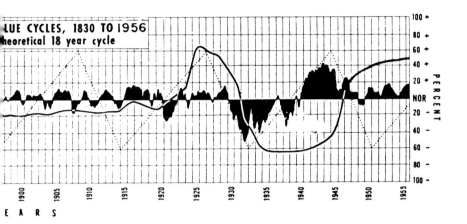

LUE CYCLES, 1830 TO 1956
heoretical 18 year cycle

twenty stages: major steps included the growth of population as a factor in a rapid rise of rents; speculation in land; the role of easy credit in stimulating the volume of construction; overbuilding; a lull in new construction; stagnation and foreclosures. Hoyt concluded that the duration of a typical cycle from peak to peak was about eighteen years. *(Fig. 156)* Focusing on residential construction in St. Louis, Roy Wenzlick observed similar stages in its real estate cycle, which lasted fifteen to twenty years. This was about three times as long as the average business cycle, which he deemed important, since the duration meant that "few people were able to apply information in one cycle to corresponding conditions in the next."[33]

Indeed, a key question about cycles is, if their pattern is so predictable, why don't people foresee the inevitable bust? This conundrum can perhaps be answered by looking more closely at the dynamics of speculation and at a typical skyscraper development.

General prosperity and easy financing underlie all booms. The usual pattern is this: big profits for buildings completed early in the cycle attract many more developers and investors into the market. Booms create their own momentum, and contrary to the simple notion of supply and demand, they can proceed somewhat independent of the net need for office space. To fill a new building, a developer need only attract tenants

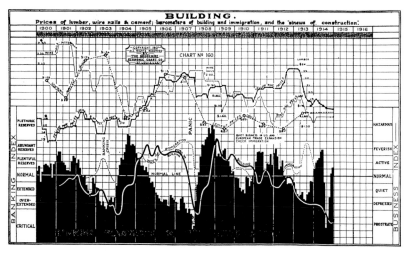

Fig. 157 Graph showing prices of various building materials, banking resources nationally, and annual building (for all types of construction). White line against black field is index of building.

from their present quarters; another's loss is his gain. Most important, though, the long lag between the conception and completion of building projects disguises the magnitude of all development until well after the supply of new space has exceeded demand. Many projects are initiated in a short span of time, until developers and lenders finally recognize that the market is glutted; then, for a number of years, there is virtually no new activity. Graphs of annual office construction show extreme curves, greater than those for other sectors of the building industry. *(Fig. 156)*

Speculating in land is a factor in all real estate cycles. Assembling buildable sites—especially one large enough to erect a profitable tower— usually required complicated negotiations with many owners or lessees. Brokers often performed this task, either for a client or on their own. In 1930, *Fortune* magazine described the skyscraper at 40 Wall Street (which became known as the Bank of Manhattan Company Building) as a model of the process of site assemblage.[34] *(Figs. 81, 158)* Keeping the scope of their plans secret so as to protect against "hold-outs," brokers would approach owners of various plots to arrange for options in the names of different companies. Title to one lot might be taken by the real estate

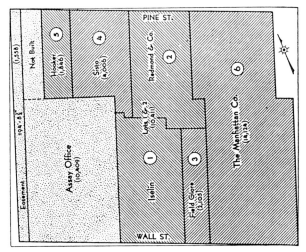

Fig. 158 Assembled lots for 40 Wall Street (Bank of Manhattan Company Building).

house for the developer; title to another would go to a corporation organized by the promoter. For 40 Wall Street there were seven lots assembled, and the strategy of the brokers was compared to a military campaign:

> The property is attacked from the principal front, and the lots facing the street—say Wall Street—are first secured. Then the secondary lots are taken. And by the time the gentleman in possession of the rear lots have begun to suspect that their properties have key value to a great scheme, they find themselves cut off from the sun and with only one possible profitable movement—backwards and out.[35]

One unified lot was usually valued at 10 percent more than the sum of its parts, though some believed that it could be worth 50 percent more. For his work, the real estate agent would receive a commission of 2.5 percent on sales up to $100,000, grading to 1 percent on sales of more than $2,000,000, a standard set by the Real Estate Board of New York.[36]

Once a site was assembled, the promoter would hire an architect to create an impressive rendering that could be sent to the newspapers with a

161

press release announcing the project. *(See Fig. 94)* Such publicity was often designed to attract a a major client or a buyer for the entire package; the plans for the Chrysler Building were sold in this manner.[37] A quick turnover could prove very lucrative. A 1930 article in *Fortune* reported that most of the "killings" in skyscraper construction were made in this way, and that profits of $1 or $2 million could be made on a $500,000 cash investment.[38] Some sites were reported to have changed hands several times before being built upon, making it possible, as the builder William Starrett noted, "to turn a profit without turning a spadeful of earth."[39]

The next step for a speculator was to negotiate a sufficient number of leases to approach lenders for construction money. The three standard sources of funds were savings banks, insurance companies, and bond houses. Savings banks offered the best rates (about 5 percent or under), but their policies were conservative and they financed a maximum of 50 or 60 percent of the value of the completed structure. The second lowest rate was offered by insurance companies (around 5.5 percent), which, like the banks, did not lend either the full value of the property or the total cost of construction. Bond houses charged higher rates (around 6 to 10 percent), but would fund the entire sum; for this reason, as well as their willingness to accept higher risk projects than the other institutions, they became the most common form of financing for speculative office buildings.[40]

Trade in bonds dealing exclusively or largely in building issues first developed in the 1890s to finance the growing demand for large commercial buildings—structures of a scale that required mortgages exceeding the borrowing capacity of most individuals.[41] Their popularity increased greatly after World War I as a result of the public's familiarity with war bonds; offered in denominations of $100, $500, and $1,000, the bonds were accessible to small investors. Loans were secured by the future value of the property. The bonds performed somewhat like preferred stocks, though the investor did not own "shares" in a particular building, but rather, in the combined portfolio of the bond house. The practice was outlined in brief by Shultz and Simmons:

OFFICE BUILDING OCCUPANCY OF THE CENTRAL BUSINESS AREA
IN NEW YORK CITY

Date of survey	Finan-cial Dist.	Insur-ance Dist.	City Hall Dist.	Grand Central Dist.	Plaza Dist.	Times Square Dist.	Colum-bus Circle Dist.	All Dist.
				Percent Occupied				
Feb. 1925	93.7	95.6	95.5	93.9				94.0
May "	90.7	95.0	94.9	93.6				91.7
Oct. "	94.7	95.2	95.1	95.4	District not previously surveyed	District not previously surveyed	District not previously surveyed	95.0
Jan. 1926	96.5	95.8	95.7	96.7				95.2
Apr. "	96.9	95.3	95.1	96.8				95.5
Oct. "	96.9	95.4	95.0	96.8				95.8
Jan. 1927	97.2	95.5	95.4	95.1				95.8
Apr. "	97.5	95.4	95.2	95.2				95.7
Oct. "	96.7	95.5	94.7	87.1				92.0
Jan. 1928	96.8	95.5	94.8	88.9				89.2
May "	96.4	95.4	95.0	90.2				93.5
Oct. "	96.9	95.8	95.2	91.0	89.3		75.0	93.6
Jan. 1929	97.8	96.8	96.7	92.8	91.2		81.6	95.3
May "	98.8	97.8	94.5	91.5	92.0		86.0	94.0
Oct. "	99.1	99.0	96.6	93.2	85.8	District not previously surveyed	93.6	95.9
Jan. 1930	99.1	97.4	94.3	93.1	85.9		92.1	95.7
May "	95.6	97.0	88.8	88.0	75.3		91.8	91.1
Sept. "	95.5	97.7	90.5	88.1	71.7		92.8	91.2
Jan. 1931	96.1	97.4	90.7	88.5	68.7		90.6	91.3
May "	87.0	85.1	86.8	82.7	57.7		87.2	83.6
Sept. "	87.1	86.3	86.2	81.7	60.6		86.0	83.5
Jan. 1932	86.7	86.9	85.0	80.2	62.1		83.1	82.7
May "	83.1	83.3	83.1	78.1	55.0		80.7	79.7
Sept. "	82.1	82.6	82.8	77.1	56.5		80.5	79.4
Jan. 1933	81.4	82.9	82.2	76.9	59.3	73.3	77.1	78.6
May "	78.3	76.2	77.0	74.8	60.6	72.0	77.8	75.8
Sept. "	78.6	75.6	78.5	75.0	66.4	76.8	75.8	76.6
Jan. 1934	78.8	75.9	78.4	72.1	64.5	78.2	74.7	75.2

Fig. 159 Office building occupancy of Central Business Area, New York, 1925 to 1934.

The theory of the bond issue was based on a gradual reduction of the principal through serial repayment or amortization of the mortgage. In easy stages, from earnings of the property, annual payments amounting to about five percent of the principal were to be made after the second year. The security behind the mortgage was the steel and stone of the building. The amount of the loan and its soundness was predicated on the estimated net income of the property.[42]

A typical bond yielded six percent, which was twice the rate paid on a commercial bank savings deposit and more than two percentage points higher than the rate offered by savings banks. With major companies such as S. W. Straus, there was minimal risk, at least through the 1910s.[43]

The system worked well as long as demand for new office space remained steady and the number of new buildings was moderate. In the mid-twenties, though, the very success of the bond houses attracted a flood of investors; in 1925, $675 million in real estate bonds were sold in the United States, more than a tenfold increase over the previous five years. In 1926, new issuances totaled nearly $1 billion.[44] Under the pressure of consumer demand for bonds and in the heady atmosphere of the skyscraper boom, even conservative bond houses relaxed their lending standards.[45] And as Shultz and Simmons observed (from their post-Depression perspective), some of the companies became mere sales agencies: "The inevitable result was that the aggressive and powerful organization, totally oblivious to the natural demand for office space due to business growth, rushed ahead with new office building construction."[46]

Speaking to the national convention of building owners and managers in 1926, NABOM President Lee Thompson Smith denounced the actions of bond houses and speculative builders in the overproduction of new office space, warning that skyscrapers were being put up "entirely through the efforts of bond houses to sell bonds, whether the buildings were needed or not." He further charged that the overproduction was being caused by speculative builders "who borrow the full cost of construction regardless of return...then sell the building at a profit and proceed to erect another somewhere else."[47] Smith, of course, represented a professional organization interested in stable office rents and property values, and thus was understandably anxious about overbuilding. His alarm—which went unheeded—was entirely accurate; by the mid 1930s, many of the bond houses were in receivership; the former paragon of the industry, S. W. Straus, defaulted on $214 million in bonds, affecting some 60,000 investors.[48] The failure of the real estate bond market was as great a scandal in the 1930s as the Savings and Loan crisis of the 1980s.

After the collapse of an inflated market, it is easy to look back on the grave errors of judgment that preceded a crash; yet the basic indicators of the twenties economy seemed to promise unimpeded growth. Pent-up demand for office space after World War I, the expanding numbers of the white-collar workforce, and the increasing per-person average for office space all fueled the building industry. Each year, the summaries of annual construction figures reported record numbers. In New York in 1924, the *Real Estate Record and Builders Guide* headlined that construction was up

130 percent over the previous year, with "Continuous Unprecedented Volume of Contracts Awarded in the Five Boroughs."[49] In 1926, contracts again exceeded all previous years, which "was a distinct surprise to close observers of the industry, many of whom in the early part of last year were firm in their belief that the high level of 1925 would seldom if ever be equalled."[50] In 1927, the market was slightly less active, but 1928 was another record year. Industry expert Charles F. Noyes asserted: "Never has the outlook been brighter and never has a more prosperous year passed for the important operators and builders than 1928."[51] The same held true for 1929.

The volume of office space constructed in New York from 1925 to 1929 was more than 17 million square feet, and projects initiated by 1930 and completed by 1933 added another 13 million, a total of 30 million square feet in eight years.[52] Through the first five years of this phenomenal expansion, low vacancy rates continued to indicate a strong market for more new office buildings. From 1925 until 1931, occupancy for first-class properties citywide averaged between ninety-one and nearly ninety-six percent (ten percent vacancy was assumed to be normal, in order to accommodate the normal pattern of leasing). The market in the financial district was particularly strong; in late 1929 and early 1930, occupancy was at ninety-nine percent.[53] By mid-1931, though, the vacancy rate had shot up to seventeen percent, and it peaked in 1934 at around twenty-five percent.[54] *(Fig. 159)*

Several factors worked together to fuel the skyscraper boom of the late 1920s. The successive years of record-breaking construction and low vacancy rates for quality properties (new buildings were filling up at the expense of some older structures), prompted both developers and financiers to ignore warnings about overbuilding. As bond houses and other institutions, flush with prosperity, competed for real estate deals, finding financing became so simple that *Fortune* opened the article on speculative building with the line: "All a man needs to own a skyscraper is the money and the land. And he may be able to get along without the money."[55] With loans secured by nothing more than the future value of the property, developers had little to lose if they failed. In retrospect, it is

Fig. 160 Lower Manhattan, tallest towers all completed between 1929 and 1931.

clear that the system was doomed at some point to catastrophic failure. But, like the stock market in 1929, most people were caught up in the fever. As Frederick Lewis Allen explained in *Only Yesterday* (1931): "As you look at the high prices recorded on September 3, 1929, remember that on that day few people imagined that the peak had actually been reached. The enormous majority fully expected the Big Bull Market to go on and on."[56]

Both building forms and the morphology of central business districts have a temporal dimension: they are shaped by the cyclical character of the real estate industry. Because escalating land prices drive up the number of stories needed to spread the cost of the lot, the tallest buildings generally appear at the end of a boom cycle. Around 1925, major New York towers averaged between thirty and forty stories, but by the end of the decade, most new buildings were forty to forty-five stories, even for quite small sites. In 1930, Clark and Kingston demonstrated that the economic height for a major building on a large site (200 x 400 feet) in a prime district had

Fig. 161 Forty-second Street towers, all completed between 1928 and 1931.

risen to sixty-three stories. The surge of construction from 1929 to 1931 saw about a dozen towers over fifty stories, including five between sixty-seven and eighty-five floors. Although precise equations for the most profitable number of stories depended on the cost of land and on anticipated rents (both of which related to location), in general, height was a barometer of a boom. The dominant towers in aerial photographs of Manhattan were almost all begun in two cyclical peaks—from 1910 to 1913 or 1928 to 1931. *(Figs. 5, 160, 161)*

Cycles also affected density and spatial distribution. Favoring proven districts, developers often squeezed very tall buildings onto small sites, greatly intensifying concentrations. *(Figs. 169, 170)* In addition, higher tax valuations on lots with skyscrapers caused an upward revaluation of adjacent properties based on their potential for multistory use; this action encouraged—or even forced—more intensive development of central areas.[57] Developers also expanded at the edges of a successful zone. As one industry expert recommended in the *Record and Guide*, following a record year for conveyances:

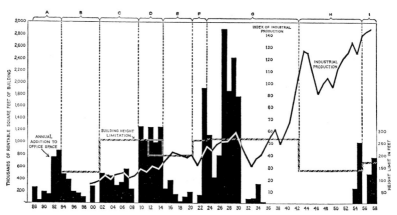

Fig. 162 Height limitation changes in Chicago.

Anyone who considers calmly the existing situation must reach the conclusion that there is no surer way of making money in the world than to
purchase improved real estate which carries itself in some central but less
expensive district of Manhattan, particularly real estate situated on an
avenue....It is the appreciation of this fact, coupled with the excellent
renting conditions, which is responsible for the current activity and
strength.[58]

In the heady optimism of booms, some speculators pioneered in new areas,
hoping that with large-scale projects, they could spawn a popular new district. This strategy failed with the Empire State, but worked at Rockefeller
Center and on Chicago's North Michigan Avenue.

The oversupply of office space produced during booms often spurred a
political reaction. Most municipal regulations were implemented during
the downturn that followed a period of extreme overproduction.[59] The
height restrictions passed in 1893 in Chicago and New York's first zoning
in 1916 were both enacted in the first phase of a real estate recession.
Conversely, in the early 1920s, when the Chicago office market experienced high demand and low vacancies, the city passed a new law that
allowed towers.

Keeping in mind the pattern of boom behavior, we can look back at major periods of construction in Chicago and New York and highlight the role of speculative development. Building booms corresponded to prosperity in the national economy, but the particular cycles in each city occurred in somewhat different times and reflected different local conditions.

Chicago's cycles were exhaustively analyzed by Homer Hoyt, who described them as being "like tidal waves in their magnitude."[60] In his view, the principal reasons for cycles were the steady pressures of population (which more than tripled between 1890 and 1930, from 1.1 million to 3.4 million residents) and real estate speculation.[61] The boom that saw the rise of the first tall office buildings began in 1879 and peaked between 1889 and 1892, the years before height regulation. As discussed in Part I, buildings of this period included such landmarks of the Chicago School as the Rookery, Manhattan, Monadnock, Masonic Temple, Reliance, Old Colony, Fisher, and Marquette Buildings; there were twenty-one speculative highrises constructed during this three-year peak, mostly financed by stock subscription.[62] The glut of new space, made worse by the depression of 1893, resulted in a downturn of construction and land values that reached a nadir in 1898; not until 1902 were the vacancies absorbed. As rents rose, there was pressure to build, but many in the real estate industry complained that the height limitation of 130 feet (about twelve stories) was not profitable, and that the regulation was hindering new construction. When the city council doubled the height limit to 260 feet in 1902, plans for eighteen new buildings were announced.[63] *(Fig. 162)*

From 1902 until around 1915, growth in the Loop was strong and steady, without the characteristic pattern of boom and bust, and without a comparable surge of speculation that hit New York in 1905–1906. Stimulated by high office rents, there was a flurry of construction in 1910, and especially in 1911, when developers raced to file permits before the deadline that once again lowered the height limit, this time to 200 feet. From 1912 through 1914, Chicago added over a million square feet of office space each year. But after the new cap took effect in 1914, construction dropped off almost completely until 1923. This occurred in part because during the war years, much real estate investment was directed into agricultural land, which doubled in value through the 1910s. This situation reversed after 1920 as population pressures and the long hiatus in construction drove up rents; in 1920, in response to this pressure, the height limit returned to 260 feet.[64]

By 1923, when the city enacted the zoning ordinance allowing a tower, land values and commercial rents had doubled in the Loop, and the boom was in full swing.[65] During the peak years of construction from 1923 to 1929, around 13 million square feet of office space was created, nearly twice its previous total.[66] The new buildings were widely distributed throughout the CBD, including in the western Loop and along the river, and on the developing commercial strip of North Michigan Avenue. For several years, the additional space was successfully absorbed by the expanding economy; in 1927, the overall vacancy rate in both new and old buildings was still under ten percent. A year later, though, many projects faced troubles with financing, and after the stock market crash in October 1929, the situation grew steadily worse. By 1931, the vacancy rate was over twenty percent.[67]

New York experienced its cyclicity on a somewhat different schedule. Growth was slow in the last years of the century, but after 1900, general business prosperity began to affect the office-building market. Speculation was rampant by 1905, when a record number of conveyances were reported, a forty percent increase over the previous year.[68] Demand for space in new buildings was strong (rents for new buildings hit a peak in 1905 at around $3.50 per square foot, while older buildings brought only about $1.75); this naturally stimulated speculative construction.[69] After several normal years, 1909 saw a record number of plans filed in Manhattan. Average growth was sustained through 1912, but the next year, the *Record and Guide* reported "an almost uninterrupted and unprecedented stagnation"; the situation worsened through 1914, the same years that Chicago enjoyed record volume.[70] Much of the new office space created in these years was concentrated in major structures such as the Adams Express, Woolworth, and Equitable Buildings.

Most construction was focused on a tight geography of the canyons of Broadway and Wall Street. It is instructive to compare a map of land values in 1903 with photographs of Lower Manhattan's densely packed skyscrapers, for both clearly illustrate the astonishing contrast in values for property separated by only a few hundred feet. *(Figs. 163, 164)* The most expensive land ($400 per square foot) was at the intersection of Wall and Broad Streets, the site of the New York Stock Exchange, and the next highest values (ranging from $350 to $250 per square foot) lined Broadway north of Trinity Church.[71] Just two blocks to the west, though, values plummeted to $25 per square foot, and down to $10 near the waterfront. The lower values were reflected in form in the great expanse of older lowrise structures from which the crowded towers rose.

Such tenfold and higher differences underscore the familiar quip that the first three rules of real estate development are "location, location, and location." Only in New York was there such a dramatic disparity in land values within a short radius. Indeed, Hurd's 1903 survey of twenty American cities showed that New York was the only one in which the value of land for office buildings was higher than for the best retail areas; prime financial land in Manhattan was valued at $35,000 per foot of frontage, while the best retail districts had values of about $18,000. The ratio was reversed in Chicago, where the costliest land, $15,000 per front foot, was used for department stores, while financial land averaged $8,000 per front foot.[72]

Value relates to the intensity of use—the human traffic or the number of occupants—and the income it can generate, either as rents or in revenues from sales. The anchor of extreme wealth in Lower Manhattan and powerful financial institutions such as the New York Stock Exchange, major banks, and corporations made both proximity for business and prestige addresses much desired, and thus drove up the price of land and the heights of buildings. This was particularly true in the late nineteenth century through the 1910s, when the first tall office buildings clustered around Broadway and Wall Street and near City Hall on Park Row, but the financial district remained a focus of development through the 1920s. Even in

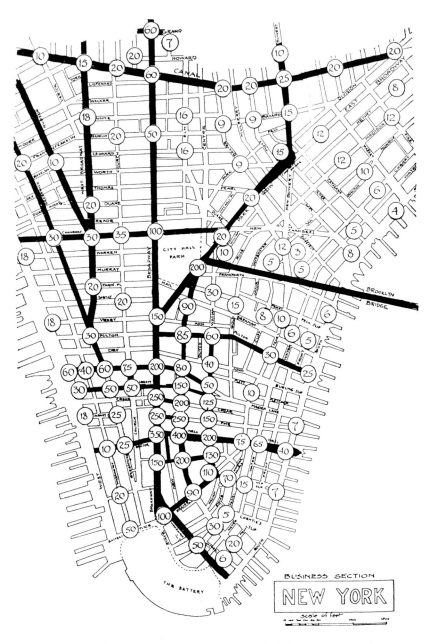

Fig. 163 Land values in Lower Manhattan (1903), dollars per square foot.

Fig. 164 Lower Manhattan looking north, c.1914; business buildings lining Broadway.

1941, a study entitled *Decentralization in New York City* gave ample reasons for the concentration in Lower Manhattan:

> Dependence on network and telegraph, telephone, and cable lines coming to a central focus has tended to tie the financial district to one spot. It is important that financial institutions remain close to the shipping lines, Sub-treasury, Federal Reserve Bank, Customs House, Clearing House, and then principal depositors such as railroads, utilities, as well as other banks so that business may be transacted speedily and directors conveniently reached for meetings. The new clearing system of inter-office confirmation of transactions by comparison "tickets" requiring running has emphasized the need for concentration. Coffee, sugar, cotton, and cocoa markets are required by Exchange rules to have bank "margin depositories" within a given radius for accepting down payment against "future" trades and hence these exchanges must stick close together in a limited area.[73]

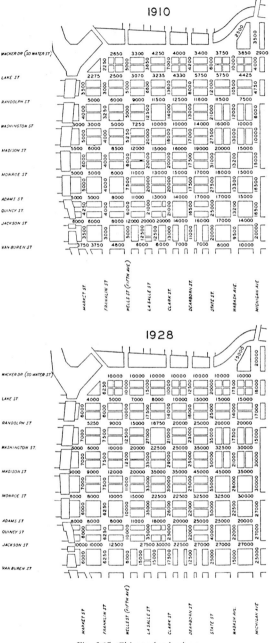

Fig. 165 Chicago land values.

Fig. 166 View south to Wacker Drive.

In the 1920s, New York spawned its second CBD, Midtown—a vaguely defined area that had the transportation nexus of Grand Central Terminal as a dominant node, and a major cross-axis on Forty-second Street. Midtown stretched north to Fifty-ninth Street and south to around Thirty-fourth Street, principally on Fifth, Madison, Park, and Lexington Avenues.[74] *(Figs. 101, 145, 161)* In the 1910s, Grand Central had spurred hotel and commercial development, but in the 1920s, office buildings became the principal use. In the last years of the decade, a battalion of new skyscrapers and residential hotels lined East Forty-second Street and marched up Lexington Avenue. *(Fig. 161)*

In Chicago, the areas devoted to office buildings spread more evenly through the Loop, and values did not show the dramatic disparities of Lower Manhattan. Hoyt compiled maps of land values for eight dates in the city's history. The years 1910 and 1928 are illustrated here; numbers refer to one foot of frontage, with a lot depth of about 160 feet, not per square foot, as in the New York map.[75] *(Fig. 165)* In 1910, the highest prices were on State Street between Madison and Monroe Streets, the area of the major department stores; these were $27,500 to $31,000 per front

Fig. 167 View from Chicago's Board of Trade, to northwest quarter of Loop.
Zoning-law towers, thirty to forty stories, were widely dispersed.

foot. In the financial district around the Board of Trade and on South
LaSalle Street, values were around $20,000, and the mix of office buildings
and hotels on southern Michigan Avenue ranged from $10,000 to
$20,000. By 1928, the numbers had risen fairly consistently throughout
the Loop, generally 50 to 100 percent above values in 1910. South LaSalle
property rose by around half, to $35,000, while at Randolph and State
Streets, values increased from around $11,800 to $25,000. Some of the
greatest gains were on Michigan Avenue: on blocks between Monroe and
Washington Streets, values elevated from $10,000 and $15,000 to
$30,000, while just south of the Michigan Avenue Bridge (opened in
1920), a group of tall towers built on relatively narrow lots created a critical mass that multiplied values sixfold and more, from around $2,500 to
$3,500 to $15,000 to $20,000. *(Fig. 170)* All of these gains were short-
lived, for by 1931, values were halved almost everywhere.

One reason for Chicago's multicentered office development may have
been the circular route of the elevated rail lines that ringed the business district. As Hoyt suggested: "A different system of transit, such as subways,
might have spread business development in a longer line....But the Loop

Fig. 168 View from New York's Chrysler Building, west across Midtown.
Towers completed between 1928 and 1931, fifty to sixty stories, crowded the Grand Central district.

land pattern was the inevitable result of a transportation system which inten-
sified the natural advantages of the Loop area."[76] The city's height restrictions also affected the spread by forcing horizontal, rather than vertical
expansion; indeed, some of the political impetus behind the original ordinance came from property owners on the edge of the business district who
hoped growth would extend their direction.[77] Most of the Loop was built
up block after block with flat-roofed boxes, ranging in height from 130 feet
to 260 feet, depending on the current regulation. Despite the City Beautiful
visions of Daniel Burnham and a generation of civic efforts, though, the
skyline never developed a strong visual order. The post-zoning towers
marked the widely dispersed points of new development, including both
ends of LaSalle Street, along the Chicago River and Wacker Drive, and
north and south on Michigan Avenue. *(Figs. 4, 6, 41, 104, 105, 166, 167)*

The question of whether municipal regulations dampened Chicago's
development—especially speculative building—was raised in Part I in connection with the discussion of the slow revival of office construction after
World War II. As we have seen, from the first ordinance in 1893, the fluc-
tuations in height limits clearly affected short-term decisions about

Fig. 169 Berenice Abbott photograph, Wall Street, 1938.
New York's skyscraper districts are far taller and more dense than Chicago's.
At left, forty-one story Bankers Trust; at center, base of seventy-story 40 Wall Street.

Fig. 170 Chicago, 1930s.
Cluster of twenties towers near Michigan Avenue Bridge.
At left, twenty-five story Tribune Tower, at center, slender spires rise around thirty stories.

construction. Shultz and Simmons argued that the restrictions "crippled" the city's growth, because at times they capped the maximum building size below the level for profitable construction. In so doing, the authors contended, Chicago lost businesses that would have liked to erect a prominent tower, both for their own use and for its advertising value; indeed, they claimed some headquarters moved to New York.[78] Their chart of Chicago's annual production of office space, the changing maximum heights, and the index of industrial production showed that, at certain points, new development lagged considerably behind the national economy. *(Fig. 162)*

The dynamics of urban growth and inter-city competition is very complicated, and their hypothesis was probably overstated. New York was vastly dominant in the U.S. economy throughout the first half of the twentieth century. In virtually every category—wholesale trade, imports and exports, banking, even manufacturing—the eastern metropolis far outranked Chicago and all other American cities.[79] It seems natural that this commanding lead would correlate in business buildings. Yet, there also seems to be something logical in the idea that when larger structures are permitted, cities grow faster.

New York profited from its aggressive speculative environment. The initial laissez-faire climate, then the liberal zoning envelope, spawned more and more, and taller and taller towers. In 1929, the planning journal *American City* took a "skyscraper census," counting all buildings of twenty-one or more stories across the country.[80] Of the total of 374, New York had 188 (with a couple of dozen more finished by 1931), while Chicago had 65. Of buildings exceeding 500 feet in 1931, Manhattan had 36, Chicago, 8. Even more impressive was New York's lead in the category of buildings of ten to twenty stories; its 2,291 to Chicago's 384 was a total larger than all other American cities combined. The net volume of office space was likewise disproportionate: between 1871 and 1923, Chicago added about 14 million square feet of office space; during the same period, New York constructed about 74 million.[81] In the boom of the 1920s and early 1930s, Chicago added 13 million square feet of office space, New York, 38 million.[82] Certainly one important factor in Manhattan's success as a business center was its vast supply of rentable space—most of it built by speculators—which ensured that the market remained highly competitive.

While New York continues to vastly outdistance Chicago in the total supply of office space (with over 316 million to 116 million square feet in 1991), the "Second City" claimed first place in one category when in the 1970s it became home to the world's tallest building, the Sears Tower. Chicago takes pride in this primacy and its history of engineering prowess, and very tall buildings have been actively encouraged by the city government. In 1989, the Planning Commission approved the proposal (now postponed) for a new record-setter, a 1914-foot, needle-thin spire to be named the Miglin-Beitler Tower after its speculative developers.[83] Such an unbashed embrace of bigness now seems characteristic of Chicago. In New York, however, professional and public opinion has shifted against great height, and several proposals for the world's tallest building, which were met with loud protests, were withdrawn.[84] Civic boosterism and local politics can create a climate of what is possible in a city and play an important role in decisions, especially at the extremes.

In general, though, buildings grow tall for a number of reasons. One, often noted by historians and social critics, is to attract attention—thus advertising the building itself, the owner, or an anchor tenant. Another impetus is the boom-bust cycle through which the real estate industry periodically answers a real demand for new office space with rampant overbuilding. Cycles tend to produce an irrational-looking pattern when seen in two dimensions as a graph of annual production or on the skyline as very tall or densely clustered towers. Over the century, critics of the skyscraper city such as Lewis Mumford have denounced urban congestion and suggested that tall buildings are only acceptable as isolated structures.[85] But that is not the nature of cities. Piling story on story only makes economic sense where land values are high—which is a condition that reflects the demand for location.

Skyscrapers are the ultimate architecture of capitalism. The first blueprint for every tall building is a balance sheet of estimated costs and returns. That bottom line is as true today as it was in 1893 when Barr Ferree noted that "a building must pay, or there will be no investor ready with money to meet its cost." Just as functional concerns, municipal codes, and individual sites affect building forms, so does the program for profit. The rise of the skyscraper and the development of downtowns cannot be interpreted without understanding the economic aspects of urban architecture. Cities are competitive commercial environments where buildings are businesses and space is a commodity. The principles that give them order are complex, but comprehensible, and in that, there is great beauty.

Notes

Introduction

1   Although a great deal has been written about skyscrapers in studies that focus on a particular city, period, or stylistic movement, there have been few attempts to offer a historical framework for periodization. By his own description, Paul Goldberger wanted his survey, *The Skyscraper* (New York: Knopf, 1981), "to put all phases of skyscraper development together into a single narrative." (ix) His story, though, plays out as an early contest between Chicago and New York and a break at mid-century with "The Triumph of Modernism." In *The Tall Building Artistically Reconsidered: The Search for a Skyscraper Style* (New York: Pantheon, 1984), Ada Louise Huxtable described the "four phases or styles" of the history of the skyscraper as "functional, eclectic, modern, and postmodern." Because the motivation for her short book (really an extended essay) was to comment on recent postmodern productions, her historical discussion is cursory and focuses almost entirely on issues of style. Throughout the literature of the skyscraper, stylistic and technological changes after World War II mark the break between eras.

2   Urban Land Institute, *Tall Office Buildings in the United States* (Washington, DC: Urban Land Institute, 1984), 9.

3   Numerous scholars have engaged in the the debate over the issue of the "first skyscraper" and whether Chicago or New York should be credited as its birthplace. This lengthy historiography has been neatly summarized by Rosemarie Haag Bletter in "The Invention of the Skyscraper: Notes on its Diverse Histories," *Assemblage* no. 2 (February 1987): 110–117. The Home Insurance Company Building, erected in 1884–85, was long considered the first tall office building erected with a rigid metal frame, and thus the grand-daddy of all steel-cage construction. Several essays in John Zukowsky, ed., *Chicago Architecture, 1872–1922* (The Art Institute of Chicago, and Munich: Prestel, 1987) discuss other precedents and more recent critical writings. Among champions of New York, the skyscraper is defined by verticality and relative height. Proponents such as Winston Weisman and Sarah Landau consider masonry structures of the 1870s such as the Tribune and Western Union Buildings either "proto-skyscrapers," or the earliest examples of the type. See in particular, Winston Weisman, "A New View of Skyscraper History," in Edgar Kaufmann, Jr., *The Rise of an American Architecture* (New York: Praeger and the Metropolitan Museum of Art, 1970), and Sarah Bradford Landau, "The Tall Office Building Artistically Reconsidered: Arcaded Buildings of the New York School, c.1870–1890," in Helen Searing, ed., *In Search of Modern Architecture: A Tribute to Henry-Russell Hitchcock* (New York: Architectural History Foundation and Cambridge: MIT Press, 1982), 136–164.

4   *Report of the Heights of Buildings Commission* (New York: Board of Estimate and Apportionment, 1913), 15; Homer Hoyt, *One Hundred Years of Land Values in Chicago* (Chicago: University of Chicago Press, 1933), 281.

5   Probably the most widely read of any account of the Chicago School was Sigfried Giedion's influential text, *Space, Time and Architecture* (Cambridge: Harvard University Press, 1941). The chief historian of the Chicago skyscraper is, of course, Carl Condit, who authored a series of books on the subject including *The Rise of the Skyscraper* (Chicago: University of Chicago Press, 1952), its later revision as *The Chicago School of Architecture* (Chicago: University of Chicago Press, 1964), and *Chicago, 1910–1929* (Chicago: University of Chicago Press, 1973). It is interesting to note that there are no plans in these books.

6   The polemical history of modernist writers has in recent years been revised by numerous scholars, incuding Robert Bruegmann in "The Marquette Building and the Myth of the Chicago School," *Threshold* (Fall 1991): 6–23, which offers a thorough discussion of the term "Chicago School" and the shifting emphasis of historians who have studied the city's highrise buildings of the late nineteenth century. On the "construction of meaning" through the sky-scraper in the late nineteenth century, see Daniel Bluestone, *Constructing Chicago* (New Haven: Yale University Press, 1991), 104–151.

7   With a focus in on New York in the 1920s, European Thomas A.P. Van Leeuwen in *The Skyward Trend of Thought* (The Hague: AHA Books, 1986) has pointed to the conflicts of American culture in the skyscraper form. Also see William R. Taylor, *In Pursuit of Gotham: Culture and Commerce in New York* (New York: Oxford University Press, 1992).

8   Paul Goldberger, *The Skyscraper*, op. cit., 24, 26.

9   Leland Roth, *A Concise History of American Architecture* (New York: Harper and Row, 1980), 187.

10   In addition to the volumes by Condit, op. cit., and The Art Institute of Chicago catalogs listed in note 11, important studies of Chicago buildings and architects include Sally A. Kitt Chappell, *Architecture and Planning of Graham, Anderson, Probst and White, 1912–1936* (Chicago: University of Chicago Press, 1992), and Robert Breugmann, ed., *Holabird and Roche and Holabird and Root: An Illustrated Catalog of Works, 1880–1940*, 3 vols. (New York: Garland, 1991). For the 1920s, most of the writing on Chicago has been dominated by the 1922 Chicago Tribune Competition; an interpretation of that event from the perspective of this study is a topic too long to deal with here, and I have avoided it.
The chief chronicler of New York buildings is Robert A.M. Stern and his various co-authors on the series, *New York 1900, New York 1930*, and *New York 1960* (see bibliography). A great deal of attention has been given to Art Deco skyscrapers of the twenties and thirties; of these sur-veys, the best is Cervin Robinson and Rosemarie Haag Bletter, *Skyscraper Style: Art Deco New York* (New York: Oxford University Press, 1975).

11   The catalog was the second documenting a pair of ambitious exhibitions, *Chicago Architecture, 1872–1922*, op. cit., and John Zukowsky, ed., *Chicago Architecture and Design, 1923–1993: Reconfiguration of an American Metropolis* (Chicago: The Art Institute of Chicago, and Munich: Prestel, 1993); my essay is "Light, Height, and Site: The Skyscraper in Chicago," 118–139.

12   Carol Hershelle Krinsky, "Sister Cities," in John Zukowsky, ed., *Chicago and New York: Architectural Interactions* (Chicago: The Art Institute of Chicago, 1984), 50–76.

13   Jane Jacobs, *The Death and Life of Great American Cities* (New York: Vintage, 1961) and Rem Koolhaas, *Delirious New York* (New York: Oxford University Press, 1978).

14   Many of Susman's best essays, ranging from 1963 through the early 1980s are collected in his only book, *Culture as History* (New York: Pantheon, 1984).

15   William Cronon, *Nature's Metropolis: Chicago and the Great West* (New York: Norton, 1991).

16   Indeed, I mention architects quite often, without crediting, clients, contractors, engineers, and other important figures at all: old habits die hard.

17   Sullivan's run-on sentences are difficult to read; my editing, I think, retains the essence. For a reprint of the original article, published in *Lippincott's* (March 1896), see Louis H. Sullivan, *Kindergarten Chats and Other Writings* (New York: Dover, 1918; reprint, 1979), 202–213; quotation, 206.

18   In another reference to the commercial nature of the office building he referred to it as: "this sterile pile, this crude, harsh, brutal agglomeration, this stark, staring exclamation of eternal strife." The architect's problem was to impart to this sterile pile "sentiment, beauty, (and) the cult of a higher life." Ibid., 202.

19   George Hill, "The Economy of the Office Building," *Architectural Record* (1904): 313.

20   Barr Ferree, "Economic Conditions of Architecture in America," in *Proceedings of the Twenty-Seventh Annual Convention of the American Institute of Architects* (Chicago: Inland Architect, 1893), 228–241; quotation, 231.

Part I

1   Gilbert's phrase, a "machine that makes the land pay" appeared in his article "The Financial Importance of Rapid Building," *Engineering Record* 41 (30 June 1900): 624. It was reintroduced by Sharon Irish in her excellent article "A Machine That Makes the Land Pay: The West Street Building in New York," *Technology and Culture* 30 (April 1989): 376–397.

2   George Hill, "Wasted Opportunities, No. III," *Architectural Record* 3 (1893): 436.

3   Statistics are quoted from an article by Kirk M. Reid, an illuminating engineer at Nela Park, Cleveland, a research center for General Electric; see "Artificial Light in Offices and Stores," *Buildings and Building Management* 25 (June 8, 1925): 43–46.

4   In contrast to the many sanitary surveys of tenement conditions and factories, there were few studies of working conditions in office buildings. On the 1916 report by the New York City Department of Health see Charles M. Nichols, ed., *Studies on Building Height Limitations in Large Cities with Special Reference to Conditions in Chicago, Proceedings of an Investigation of Building Height Limitations Conducted Under the Auspices of the Zoning Committee of the Chicago Real Estate Board, Zoning Committee of the Chicago Real Estate Board in 1923* (Chicago: The Chicago Real Estate Board, 1923), 34–36. Hereafter, *Building Height Limitations.* Statistics from the 1920s appeared in Reid, "Artificial Light in Offices and Stores," op. cit.: 43–44.

5   Earle Shultz and Walter Simmons, *Offices in the Sky* (Indianapolis: Bobbs-Merrill, 1959), 202–203.

6   Hill, "Wasted Opportunities," op. cit.: 437 and Hill, "Some Practical Conditions in the Design of the Modern Office Building," *Architectural Record* 2 (1893): 471.

7   A chart of average rents for spaces of various depths was prepared by Boston building manager W. H. Ballard in 1923 and was reprinted by Shultz and Simmons, *Offices in the Sky*, op. cit., 131.

8   Harvey Wiley Corbett, "New Stones for Old," *Saturday Evening Post* 198 (15 May 1926): 17.

9   The industry journal *Buildings and Building Management*, which began publication in 1913, ran many articles on efficient office planning and regularly included a supplement, *Skyscraper News.*

10   Shultz and Simmons, *Offices in the Sky*, op. cit., 130.

11   Ibid.

12   Ibid.

13   Aldis 's eight fundamentals are reprinted in Shultz and Simmons, *Offices in the Sky*, op. cit., 33–35. Also see Miles Berger, *They Built Chicago: Entrepreneurs Who Shaped a Great City's Architecture* (Chicago: Bonus Books, 1992), 39–48.

14   Barr Ferree, *The Modern Office Building* (New York: privately printed, 1896), 32.

15   On tall buildings in New York in the late nineteenth century, see Winston Weisman, "A New View of Skyscraper History," in Edgar Kaufmann, Jr., *The Rise of an American Architecture* (New York: Praeger and the Metropolitan Museum of Art, 1970); Kenneth Turney Gibbs, *Business Architectural Imagery in America, 1870–1930* (Ann Arbor: University of Michigan Research Press, 1984); and Mona Domosh, *Scrapers of the Sky: The Symbolic and Functional Structures of Lower Manhattan.* Ph.D., Department of Geography, Clark University, MA (1985). A major study on New York skyscrapers to 1914 by Carl Condit and Sarah Bradford Landau is forthcoming from Yale University Press.

16   William Birkmire, *The Planning and Construction of High Office-Buildings* (New York: John Wiley & Sons, 2nd ed., 1900), 7.

17   A key motive of the platting was to facilitate real estate development. Some lots were fifteen feet wide, but twenty-five feet was most common; this was a good size for residential construction, the use envisioned at the time. See Edward K. Spann, "The Greatest Grid: The New York Plan of 1811," in Daniel Schaeffer, ed., *Two Centuries of American Planning* (Baltimore: Johns Hopkins, 1988), 11–39.

18   Dimensions for all buildings to 1899 are taken from *Atlas of the City of New York, Borough of Manhattan* vol. 1 (Philadelphia: G. W. Bromley and Company, 1899). For later structures, the major source was *Manhattan Land Book* (Pelham, NY: Sanborn, 1955).

19   Quoted in "The Liberty Tower," New York City Landmarks Preservation Commission, Designation List, LP1243.

20   On the Metropolitan Life Insurance Building, see Gail Fenske and Deryck Holdsworth, "Corporate Identity and the Modern Office Building, 1895–1915," in David Ward and Olivier Zunz, eds., *The Landscape of Modernity* (New York: Russell Sage, 1992), 139–142; and "Metropolitan Life Insurance Company Tower," New York City Landmarks Preservation Commission, Designation List 217, LP-1530.

21   *The Metropolitan Life Building, New York*. Privately printed publicity pamphlet, c.1909.

22   On the costs and returns of the Equitable see C.T. Coley, "Method of Checking Economical Height of Office Buildings," *Buildings and Building Management* 13 (July 1913): 41–47, and on the speculative deal, see Louis J. Horowitz, *The Towers of New York* (New York: Simon and Schuster, 1937), 133–166. The poor rental performance of the Woolworth Building was discussed in Nichols, *Building Height Limitations*, op. cit., 24.

23   There were numerous contemporary studies and articles on figuring economic height; for example, see George Hill, "The Economy of the Office Building," *Architectural Record* 15 (April 1904): 326; and C.T. Coley, "Method of Checking Economical Height of Office Buildings," *Engineering Record* 68 (5 July 1912): 21–22 and Coley, op. cit., note 22.

24   See Sally A. Kitt Chappell, "A Reconsideration of the Equitable Building in New York," *Journal of the Society of Architectural Historians* LXIX (March 1990): 106, and Chappell, *Architecture and Planning of Graham, Anderson, Probst and White, 1912–1936* (Chicago: University of Chicago Press, 1992), 104–111. The measure of good elevator service was perceptual; in New York, tenants expected service within thirty seconds. For a discussion of these issues, see C.T. Coley, "A Method for Checking the Economical Height of an Office Building," (1924) op. cit.: 42–43.

25   Also compare the three buildings with the Illinois Continental and Commercial Bank in Chicago.

26   Nichols, *Building Height Limitations*, op. cit., 70. Similarly, in their 1955 history of the office building industry, Shultz and Simmons noted that the majority of the city's buildings erected up to 1920 were of the "O" plan; see *Offices in the Sky*, op. cit., 132.

27   On the platting of Chicago, see Homer Hoyt, *One Hundred Years of Land Values in Chicago* (Chicago: University of Chicago Press, 1933), 427–428; and Harold M. Mayer and Richard C. Wade, *Chicago: Growth of a Metropolis* (Chicago: University of Chicago Press, 1969), 12, 21, 37.

28   Nichols, *Building Height Limitations*, op. cit., passim.

29   For example, the Schiller, Ashland, Columbus Memorial, Unity, and Old Colony Buildings, and the Monadnock Block all rose sixteen or more stories. In New York, the tallest buildings were the World, Manhattan Life, Home Life Insurance, and American Surety Buildings. Sources for my own count of New York buildings are Birkmire, *The Planning and Construction of High Office-Buildings*, op. cit., and Mona Domosh, *Scrapers of the Sky*, op. cit.

30   On the innovations of the city's architects and engineers, see Carl Condit, *The Rise of the Skyscraper* (Chicago: University of Chicago Press, 1952) and *The Chicago School of Architecture* (Chicago: University of Chicago Press, 1964).

31   As recounted by an associate, Owen Aldis stated that the southern, steel section of the Monadnock Block had fifteen percent more rental space, was fifteen percent lighter, and cost fifteen percent less than the northern, masonry section; see page 64 of the typescript memoir, "Recollections," by Edward A. Renwick, which is in the collection of the Ryerson and Burnham Libraries of The Art Institute of Chicago.

32   Donald Hoffmann, *The Architecture of John Wellborn Root* (Chicago: University of Chicago Press, 1973), 196–198.

33   Ibid., 67.

34   Shultz and Simmons, *Offices in the Sky*, op. cit., 273; and Nichols, *Building Height Limitations*, op. cit., 14.

35   Lot dimensions: Frank A. Randall, *History of the Development of Building Construction in Chicago* (Urbana: University of Illinois Press, 1949) and Birkmire, *The Planning and Construction of High Office-Buildings*, op. cit.

36   Owen Aldis wrote to Peter Brooks that the Monadnock contained sixty-eight percent rentable area, as opposed to the Rookery, with fifty to fifty-five percent, or the Home Insurance, with forty-five percent; see Hoffmann, *The Architecture of John Wellborn Root*, op. cit., 160.

37   Sources for dimensions: Randall, *History of Development and Building Construction in Chicago*, op. cit., and Birkmire, *The Planning and Construction of High Office-Buildings*, op. cit.

38   Nichols, *Building Height Limitations*, op. cit., see fold-out map insert.

39   A plan with offices on the interior court could increase rentable areas from fifty to eighty percent. However, interior offices were of secondary value, especially on the lower stories, so rental income rose by only thirty to forty percent; see Shultz and Simmons, *Offices in the Sky*, op. cit., 132.

40   For a fine analysis of the building's aesthetic features and illustrations see Bluestone, *Constructing Chicago*, op. cit., 124, 135, 140. The comment by John J. Flinn, in *Chicago, the Marvelous City of the West* (Chicago: The Standard Guide Company, 1892), 570, is cited by Bluestone, 135. Unfortunately, the open space at the Chamber of Commerce Building had to be interrupted by wire nets strung across the void to prevent suicides. Another example of an open court was the seven-story Chicago, Burlington, and Quincy Office Building (1882–83); see Hoffmann, *The Architecture of John Wellborn Root*, op. cit., 30–31.

41   Hoffmann, *The Architecture of John Wellborn Root*, op. cit., 196. Bluestone published floor plans and photos of the Masonic Temple court in *Constructing Chicago*, op. cit., 136–138.

42   Plans of these buildings appear in Ernest R. Graham, *The Architectural Work of Graham, Anderson, Probst and White* (London: Batsford, 1933).

43   See Cecil C. Evers, *The Commercial Problem in Buildings* (New York: The Real Estate Record and Builders Guide, 1914), 185. Evers explained: "In the financial sections of the larger cities, the ground floor is of considerably greater value than the upper floors, due to its greater accessibility and prominence. Thus in the financial section of New York City, where the rentals of the upper floors range from $4 per square foot per annum down to $2, that of the ground floor will be from $10 to $25, or over, or from five to six times as much as the floors above." This point is further discussed in Part II.

44   Bluestone, *Constructing Chicago*, op. cit., ch. 4.

45   Plans for this type building can be elusive: good sources include Graham, *The Architectural Work of Graham, Anderson, Probst and White*, op. cit.; Hoffmann, *The Architecture of John Wellborn Root*, op. cit.; Franz Winkler, "Some Chicago Buildings Represented by the Work of Holabird and Root," *Architectural Record* 31 (April 1912): 313–387, and the special issue "Daniel H. Burnham and His Associates" in *Architectural Record* 38 (July 1915). The internal light court was also a feature of in some department stores, most spectacularly at Marshall Fields.

46   There were a few buildings with a light court on the street, including the Woman's Temple, the New Burnham Building, and the Garland Building, but this solution is surprisingly rare considering the efficiency of the plan.

47   The "U" was advantageous for sites such as that of the Ashland Block (80 x 140 feet) and the Unity Building (80 x 150 feet). The same benefits accrued from an L-shaped plan, which was generally used on narrower lots, as in the Tacoma Building or Columbus Memorial.

48   Schultz and Simmons, *Offices in the Sky*, op. cit., 132–133.

49   I have discussed the effects of the zoning envelope on skyscraper design and visionary urbanism in two articles: "Zoning and Zeitgeist: The Skyscraper City in the 1920s," *Journal of the Society of Architectural Historians* (March 1986): 47–59; and "A 3-D CBD: How the 1916 Zoning Law Shaped Manhattan's Central Business Districts," in Todd W. Bressi, ed., *Planning and Zoning New York City, Yesterday, Today, and Tomorrow* (New Brunswick: Center for Urban Policy Research, Rutgers University, 1993), 3–26.

50   There are two outstanding accounts of the 1916 zoning resolution: S. J. Makielski, Jr., *The Politics of Zoning* (New York: Columbia University Press, 1966) and Seymour L. Toll, *Zoned American* (New York: Grossman, 1969).

51   Articles by prominent architects that advocated regulating tall buildings included: Thomas Hastings, "High Buildings and Good Architecture," *American Architect and Building News* (17 November 1894): 67–68; and Ernest Flagg, "The Dangers of High Buildings," *Cosmopolitan* 21 (May 1896): 70–79 and "The Limitation of Height and Area of Buildings in New York," *American Architect and Building News* (15 April 1908): 125–127.

52   For further discussion of earlier efforts of architects and reformers to regulate the sky-scraper, see my articles "Zoning and Zeitgeist" and "A 3-D CBD," both, op. cit.

53   For figures on the building industry, see "A Review and a Prospect," *The Real Estate Record and Builders Guide* (6 January 1912): 5–6, and "Real Estate Review and Prospect," *The Real Estate Record and Builders Guide* (2 January 1915): 3–4, hereafter referred to as *Record and Guide*.

54   Marc Weiss has analyzed the support given zoning by the real estate and financial com-munities in "Density and Intervention: New York's Planning Traditions," in Ward and Zunz, eds., *The Landscape of Modernity*, op. cit., 46–75. Also relevant is another article by Weiss, "The Politics of Real Estate Cycles," *Business and Economic History* 20 (1991): 1–8. In it, he identifies a cyclical pattern to political efforts to regulate the building industry in which calls for reform are initiated during a downturn or the early phases of an upturn, never during the boom. The theory fits the situation in New York in 1913–1916.

55   Toll, *Zoned American*, op. cit., 48.

56   Chappell, "A Reconsideration of the Equitable Building in New York," op. cit.: 90–95.

57   The exemplary leasing strategy was described in an article by the renting manager, Thomas Morch, in "The Old Equitable and the New," *Buildings and Building Management* 13 (December 1913): 26–27.

58   Toll, *Zoned American*, op. cit., 71. Also see Keith Revell, "Regulating the Landscape: Real Estate Values, City Planning, and the 1916 Zoning Ordinance," in Ward and Zunz, *The Landscape of Modernity*, op. cit., 19–45.

59   See *The Final Report of the Commission on Building Districts and Restrictions* (New York: Board of Estimate and Apportionment, 1916).

60   The specific guidelines were drafted by George B. Ford, an architect and engineer who served as the secretary for the Heights of Buildings Commission as well as a consultant to the Commission on Building Districts and Restrictions and the Planning Committee. The five basic formulas were:

1	x	width of street = 1 ft. setback : 2 ft. vertical rise
1.25	x	width of street = 1 ft. setback : 2.5 ft. vertical rise
1.5	x	width of street = 1 ft. setback : 3 ft. vertical rise
2	x	width of street = 1 ft. setback : 4 ft. vertical rise
2.5	x	width of street = 1 ft. setback : 5 ft. vertical rise

Virtually all of Manhattan was liberally zoned as one-and-one-half, two, or two-and-one-half times districts. Area districts regulated the lot coverage, the portion of the rear or sides of the lot that was kept open in yards or courts; there were five area districts, A through E. See George B. Ford, *New York City Building Zone Resolution* (New York: New York Title and Mortgage Company, 1920).

61   For a professional's description of how the zoning law generated setback forms, with 120 Wall Street as one example, see James B. Newman, "Factors in Office Planning," *Architectural Forum* 52 (June 1930): 881–890. Newman was an architect in the firm of Ely Jacques Kahn.

62   Lot dimensions for sites and areas of tower floors are taken from Yale Robbins, Inc., *Manhattan Office Buildings* (New York: Midtown, 1983) or the *Manhattan Land Book* (1955).

63   Walter H. Kilham, Jr. "Tower Floor Plans of New York Skyscrapers Compared," *American Architect* 138 (October 1930): 76.

64   Today, "Art Deco" is the common label for modernistic design of the 1920–1930s; in the period, there were numerous other terms, including "the new architecture," "setback style," "New York style," or simply, "modern." I discuss the emerging aesthetic of simple, sculptural mass and the language used to describe the new forms at length in "Zoning and Zeitgeist," op. cit.

65   A contemporary summary of "our architecture of mass" appeared in Douglas Haskell, "Building or Sculpture?" *Architectural Record* 67 (1930): 366–368.

66   Ely Jacques Kahn,"Our Skyscrapers Take Simple Forms," *New York Times* (2 May 1926): Sec. 4: 11. Also see Kahn, "The Office Building Problem in New York," *Architectural Forum* 41 (September 1924): 94.

67   Harvey Wiley Corbett, "The Planning of Office Buildings," *Architectural Record* 41 (September 1924): 90.

68   Kilham, "Tower Floor Plans of New York Skyscrapers Compared," op. cit.: 78.

69   R. H. Shreve, "The Empire State Building Organization," *Architectural Forum* 52 (June 1930): 772.

70   Arthur Loomis Harmon, "The Design of Office Buildings," *Architectural Forum* 52 (June 1930): 819.

71   Shultz and Simmons, *Offices in the Sky*, op. cit., 139.

72   Albert Kahn, "Designing Modern Office Buildings," *Architectural Forum* 52 (June 1930): 775; Harmon, "The Design of Office Buildings," op. cit.: 819.

73   Corbett, "The Planning of Office Buildings," op. cit., 90.

74   R. H. Shreve, "The Economic Design of Office Buildings," *Architectural Record* 67 (1930): 352; this article is a thorough and extremely clear statement of the issues.

A similar description was advanced by the "scientific planner" William Gompert: "The ideal office is 18 x 25 feet. The fenestration should be arranged so that it would be possible to sub-divide the 18-foot office unit into two parts to provide two small offices, each with a window, and in the back of the two offices approximately 15 x 18 feet, to have a small anteroom. This unit lends itself readily to the requirements of the small tenant;" see William H. Gompert, "Planning Office Buildings for Maximum Returns," *Record and Guide* 126 (27 December 1930): 5.

75   Walter H. Kilham, Jr. analyzed the advantages of various arrangements in "Tower Floor Plans of New York Skyscrapers Compared," op. cit.: 30–31, 76–78.

76   Corbett, "The Planning of Office Buildings," op. cit.: 92.

77   According to *Fortune*, the net rentable area of the Empire State was 1,921,811 square feet, and the gross area was approximately 2,158,000 square feet, a ratio of 69:100. The ratio of cubic foot to per square foot of rentable space was 16.11:1. See "Paper Spires," *Fortune* 1 (September 1930): 119, 122. Large buildings generally had less efficient ratios because of the large areas devoted to circulation.

78   W. C. Clark and J. L. Kingston, *The Skyscraper: A Study in the Economic Height of Modern Office Buildings* (New York: American Institute of Steel Construction, Inc., 1930). The study and book were sponsored by the AISC; R. H. Shreve served on the committee.

79   Ibid., 15.

80   Ibid., 25.

81   Ibid., table II, 25, 29. A real estate rule of thumb held that land and building costs should be at least equal; usually the building's value was greater.

82   In addition to the 60- to 70-story towers already noted, in late 1929, the first plans for the new Metropolitan Life Building proposed an 80- or 100-story tower (depending on the source), and the real estate broker Charles Noyes announced plans for a 100-story building.

83   For a more detailed discussion of the finances and design of the Empire State Building and extensive archival references, see my article "Form Follows Finance: The Empire State Building and the Forces that Shaped It," in Ward and Zunz, *The Landscape of Modernity*, op. cit., 160–187.

84   "Waldorf-Astoria Hotel in the Year's Largest Sale: Celebrated Hostelry is to Be Replaced by Fifty-Story Office Building Representing Investment of Approximately $25,000,000," *Record and Guide* 122 (29 December 1928): 7–8. Several sources called the project an office building, but William F. Lamb, described this first design as a "loft-type" building in his article, "The Empire State Building: The General Design," *Architectural Forum* 53 (January 1930): 7.

85   As recounted by the general contractor, Paul Starrett, Brown had put down $100,000 "earnest money" for an option on the property and contracted to pay $2,500,000 in cash in the first two installments for the hotel and land. Although he met the first payment, he defaulted on the second. See Starrett, *Changing the Skyline* (New York: Whittlesey House, 1938), 285.

The letter from Raskob to Kaufman is in the archives of the Hagley Museum and Library, Wilmington, Delaware, Longwood MS, 229-15, Box 1 of 5, file 26, 1. Attached to this letter is the page illustated as Fig. 95. A copy in Pierre du Pont's files includes his handwritten annotations of the sums to be paid by the different investors (lower right); of the $10,000,000 of equity (preferred stock), du Pont and Raskob were to contribute half, with the remainder to be raised by Kaufman and his associates. For the $12,500,000 needed for the second mortgage, du Pont and Raskob would jointly underwrite $1,250,000, Kaufman et al. an equal amount, and the remaining $10,000,000 to be taken by the Chatham and Phoenix affiliate. There is extensive archival material on financial aspects of the Empire State Building at Hagley in the papers of John Jacob Raskob and Pierre S. Du Pont.

86   Letter from Raskob to Kaufman, 28 August 1929, op. cit. The only reference to the scale of the project came in Raskob's remark at the end of the letter: "I appreciate the opportunity you have given us in this matter and particularly in the privilege of being associated with you and your group in the doing of something big and really worth while. I am sure it will be the most outstanding thing in New York and a credit to the city and state as well as to those associated with it." In the context of the entire letter, Raskob's comment seems to me to express optimism, but hardly a hubristic compulsion to erect the world's tallest tower.

87   The first estimate for the combined costs of $1.00 per cubic foot was, in fact, not far off the reported final costs of $1.03. The contract from Starrett Bros. signed in November 1929, was for $27 million (plus their fee of $500,000); the first figure, divided by 34 million cubic feet, equals about $.79. The $1.03 quoted by Shultz and Simmons, probably included other costs such as interest, commissions, mortgages, etc.; *Offices in the Sky*, op. cit., 168.

88   Real estate advisor Hamilton Weber noted this problem in his report to the directors. He warned: "Being primarily a renting man, I am cautious not to let mere assertion take the place of sound reason. It is difficult to give assurance that the figures for the operating statement are what might be expected...for we have absolutely no precedent to go by;" letter from Hamilton H. Weber to Robert C. Brown, 21 October 1929, Hagley Museum and Library, Longwood MS, 229-15, Box 1 of 5, folder 26, I.

89   "Paper Spires," op. cit.: 122. This article contains an excellent analysis of the financing of the Empire State Building; it was the third of in a series of six informative articles on skyscrapers published in *Fortune* from July through December 1930.

90   Veteran skyscraper designers, Shreve and Lamb had built a number of the city's towers, including, in 1926, the New York headquarters for General Motors, of which Raskob was an executive. They signed a contract on September 20, 1929. Paul Starrett described how he won the bid for the Empire State commission in *Changing the Skyline*, op. cit., 289, 292.

91   William F. Lamb, "The Empire State Building: The General Design," *Architectural Forum* 53 (January 1930): 1.

92   Ibid.: 5.

93   The land and lease buyouts for the Empire State were slightly more than $200 per square foot, which was the amount estimated for the hypothetical skyscraper in Clark and Kingston's calculations of economic height (with the recommended sixty-three stories). In later years, one of the corporation directors, Robert C. Brown, recalled that Andrew Eken of Starrett Brothers

and the architects had reported the seventy-five- and eighty-story recommendations. Notes by Robert C. Brown in response to questions posed by lawyers in regard to a law suit of 1937; Hagley Museum and Library, Raskob files, Acc. 473, file 743. Other than these notes, no specific explanation for the number of stories was included in the corporation's financial records.

R. H. Shreve discussed the general reasoning behind decisions about building height, as they related to elevator service in "The Economic Design of Office Buildings," op. cit.: 359.

94   Irwin Clavan, ""The Empire State Building: The Mooring Mast," *Architectural Forum* 54 (February 1931): 229–234. Receipts for the observatory started strong, mounting at a rate of $100,000 a month in 1931; "Observatory Tower Report," 8 June 1931, Hagley Museum and Library, Longwood Manuscripts 229-15, Box 1 of 5, file 52, III.

95   J. L. Edwards, "The Empire State Building: The Structural Frame," *Architectural Forum* 53 (August 1930): 241–246.

96   R. H. Shreve, "The Empire State Building: The Window-Spandrel-Wall Detail and its Relation to Building Progress," *Architectural Forum* 53 (July 1930): 99.

97   Ibid.: 104.

98   For example, an early proposal for a department store on the Fifth Avenue side was abandoned because Starrett argued that the special structural requirements would cause delays; "Paper Spires," op. cit.: 122.

99   Shreve, "The Economic Design of Office Buildings," op. cit.: 345–347.

100   "Paper Spires," op. cit.: 119.

101   Curtain-wall glass had not been sufficiently perfected in the 1920s, but in any case, until 1937 New York's building code required fireproof (i.e. masonry or metal) spandrels.

102   Walter Kilham noted Hood's preference for towers in the monograph *Raymond Hood, Architect* (New York: Architectural Book Publishing Co., 1973).

103   Kilham, "Tower Floor Plans of New York Skyscrapers Compared," op. cit.: 91–103.

104   I use the familiar name Rockefeller Center here, although during 1931–1932, the complex was variously known as Radio City and Rockefeller City, and the RCA Building (currently the GE Building) was called "the central tower"; see, for example, Raymond Hood, "The Design of Rockefeller City," *Architectural Forum* 56 (January 1932): 1–12. For an analysis of the roles of Hood and the other architects of the design team and for other documentation of the development see the authoritative study of Carol Hershelle Krinsky, *Rockefeller Center* (New York: Oxford University Press, 1978).

105   The form was unprecedented at the time, but became popular in the 1950s when it was generally sheathed in metal and glass or glass curtain wall. Winston Weisman and William Jordy, for example, described the RCA Building as a "slab," while Hood once referred to it as a "slat."

106 Hood, "The Design of Rockefeller City," op. cit.: 5. Krinsky uses the measurement of 27 feet 6 inches, which according to Reinhard was the dimension of the steel span.

107 This was one of the questions posed and answered by Reinhard in his article "What is the Rockefeller Radio City?" *Architectural Record* 69 (April 1931): 281.

108 G. H. Edgell, *American Architecture of Today* (New York: Charles Scribner's Sons, 1928), 356.

109 For example, the Penobscot and Fisher Buildings in Detroit, the Telephone Building in St. Louis, the Koppers Building in Pittsburgh, and the Pacific Telephone and Telegraph Building in San Francisco.

110 In 1902, the city raised the limit to 260 feet, then in 1911 reduced it to 200 feet, only to return it to 260 feet in 1920. See Nichols, *Building Height Limitations*, op. cit., and Shultz and Simmons, *Offices in the Sky*, op. cit., 285. The precise political reasons for the raising and lowering need detailed study; however, given the close correlation of real estate cycles and the lifting or lowering of the cap, it seems reasonable to assume that this was an important factor.

111 This growth was interrupted by a few minor recessions and spurts of activity, as the chart of office space production (Fig. 162) demonstrates. Shultz and Simmons, *Offices in the Sky*, op. cit., note 7, 285. On rising rents, see Homer Hoyt, *One Hundred Years*, op. cit., 238.

112 For a simplified discussion of financing methods, see Starrett, *Skyscrapers and the Men Who Build Them*, op. cit., and for Chicago, see Hoyt, *One Hundred Years*, op. cit., 237, 385, 445–446. As Hoyt noted, the credit operations of banks and bond houses tended to exaggerate the extravagances of real estate booms and depressions rather than countervail them. (446)

113 The architect Andrew Rebori described the new law in "Zoning Skyscrapers in Chicago," *Architectural Record* 58 (July 1925): 89. In a commercial district:

> If the area of a building is reduced so that above the street line height limit it covers in the aggregate not more than twenty-five percent of the area of the premises, the building above such height shall be exempted from the volume and street line height regulations. The aggregate volume in cubic feet of all such portions of the building shall not exceed one-sixth of the volume of the building as permitted by this ordinance on the premises upon which such portions are erected: provided that each one percent of the width of the lot on the street line height limit is greater in length than fifty percent of the width of the lot, such wall shall be erected not near-er to such street line than one foot; and further provided that for each ten feet in height that any such portion of the building is erected above the street line height limit, such portion of the building shall be set back one foot from all lines of adja-cent premises.
>
> In a 5th Volume District, above 264 feet, an additional volume had to be set back within a diagonal plane of thirty degrees for a distance of thirty-two feet up the slope; there was a different angle for setbacks on the back side, requiring one foot set back from the center line of the alley for each additional ten feet in height."

114 For example, a tower of 80 x 80 feet erected on a full quarter-block lot such as that of the Rookery (168 x 171 feet) could only rise only seventeen stories above the base.

115 Thoroughly discussed by Sally Chappell in *Architecture and Planning of Graham, Anderson, Probst and White*, op. cit., are the Federal Reserve Bank, 130–132; the Illinois Merchants Bank, 44–49 and 142–144; and the Builders Building, 188–189.

116 The design of the Straus Building (now the Britannica Center) was extensively documented, including various experiments with massing, facade treatments, and plans, in Leo J. Sheridan and W. C. Clark, "Perfecting the Plans of the New Straus Building," *Buildings and Building Management* 25 (16 February 1925): 31. Oddly, the tower did not fill the envelope allowed under the new zoning, and the decision to keep it relatively low seemed to have been aesthetic. See Chappell, *Architecture and Planning of Graham, Anderson, Probst and White*, op. cit., 158–162.

117 The designs for the Straus Building were the first submitted to a newly created body of NABOM, the Building Planning Service, which produced a series of articles that appeared in *Buildings and Building Management* during 1925. For the quotation, "as nearly perfect..." see Leo J. Sheridan and W. C. Clark, "Developing the Organization for Planning, Constructing, Renting, and Operating the New Straus Building," *Buildings and Building Management* 25 (5 January 1925): 31.

118 Sheridan and Clark, "Perfecting the Plans of the New Straus Building," op. cit.: 38.

119 Sheridan and Clark, "Developing the Organization for Planning, Constructing, Renting, and Operating the New Straus Building," op. cit.: 31.

120 Leo J. Sheridan and W. C. Clark, "The Advertising and Educational Campaign, Straus Building, Chicago," *Buildings and Building Management* 25 (31 August 1925): 25–32.

121 See "The Pittsfield Building," *Buildings and Building Management* 26 (2 August 1926): 31–36. The building is also described by Sally Chappell in *Architecture and Planning of Graham, Anderson, Probst and White*, op. cit., 185–187. Stores were perfectly suited to exploit the court space, since they did not require exterior windows and generally brought higher rates than offices. The interior court suited to the needs of medical professionals who preferred well-lighted, quiet, and relatively shallow offices; all space in the building was twenty-two feet or less from a window.

122 Erected after the Straus Building on a lot of comparable size, the Jewelers Building had a twenty-three-story base and seventeen-story tower. Aside from the novel parking, the design was oddly retardataire, especially in its lavish terra-cotta ornament. See Pauline A. Saliga, ed., *The Sky's the Limit: A Century of Chicago Skyscrapers* (New York: Rizzoli, 1990), 112–113. For a discussion of skyscraper garages, see R. Steven Sennott, "Forever Inadequate to the Rising Stream: Dream Cities, Automobiles, and Urban Street Mobility in Central Chicago," in John Zukowsky, ed., *Chicago Architecture and Design, 1923–1993* (Chicago: The Art Institute of Chicago, and Munich: Prestel, 1993), 62.

123 Both the Foreman State Bank and the Civic Opera buildings were by the firm of Graham, Anderson, Probst and White. See Chappell, *Architecture and Planning of Graham, Anderson, Probst and White*, op. cit., 14–23, 213–214, 218–222. The Chicago Civic Opera Building is discussed in Jane Clark's essay in Saliga, ed., *The Sky's the Limit*, op. cit., 152.

124 An excellent source for photographs and background on these buildings is Pauline Saliga's *The Sky's the Limit*, op. cit.

125 Holabird and Root was the successor of the firm of Holabird and Roche. On their practice see Robert Breugmann, ed., *Holabird and Roche and Holabird and Root: An Illustrated Catalog of Works, 1880–1940*, 3 vols. (New York: Garland, 1991) hereafter, *H & R Catalog*.

126 For documents on the Board of Trade see Breugmann, *H & R Catalog*, op. cit., vol. 3, 23–39; also see George R. Bailey, "Developing a Commanding Site in Chicago's Financial District," *Buildings and Building Management* 30 (25 August 1930): 49–61.

127 On the development of North Michigan Avenue, see John Staemper, *Chicago's North Michigan Avenue: Planning and Development, 1900–1930* (Chicago: University of Chicago Press, 1991).

128 On the Palmolive Building see Breugmann, *H & R Catalog*, op. cit., vol. 2, no. 1160, 414–424; "monument to cleanliness," 415.

129 "Selling Office Space in a New Building Outside the Central Business District," *Buildings and Building Management* 29 (15 July 1929): 30–31.

130 "The Palmolive Building," rental brochure, uncataloged files, the Ryerson and Burnham Libraries of The Art Institute of Chicago. The brochure lists tenants as of August 1930.

131 The areas for the various floors were published in Henry Hoskins, "The Palmolive Building, Chicago," *Architectural Forum* 52 (May 1930): 656. My calculations show that the total area of the tower (floors 23 through 37) was about 58,000 square feet, which was equal to one-sixth of the volume of a base section built out to the maximum envelope.

132 "The Palmolive Building," rental brochure, op. cit.

133 References to Chicago's "setback skyscrapers," or a similar phrase is common; for example, in Robert Bruegmann, "The Tribune Competition: The 1920s Metropolis," *Inland Architect* 24 (June 1980): 21.

134 Chappell, *Architecture and Planning of Graham, Anderson, Probst and White*, op. cit., 59–62, 217. Contracts for the project were signed in 1929; construction went forward in stages through the early years of the Depression and was completed in 1934.

135 The proportions of overbuilding had been even greater in New York than in Chicago; from 1925 to 1931, Manhattan had increased its total volume of office space by ninety-two percent; Chicago had grown by seventy-four percent. See the table in Shultz and Simmons, *Offices in the Sky*, op. cit., 162. Also see Robert Moore Fisher, "The Boom in Office Buildings: An Economic Study of the Past Two Decades," *Technical Bulletin* 58 (Washington, DC: Urban Land Institute, 1969): 6.

136 For example, much of the Merchandise Mart was converted to office use; see Shultz and Simmons, *Offices in the Sky*, op. cit., 286.

137 Ibid., 281, 287. This calculation assumed a ceiling height of thirteen feet.

138 Shultz and Simmons asserted: "During the period [of the late 1940s and early 1950s], New York could and did build office buildings to house the great expansion of business. Some of this business wanted to come to Chicago and would have if it could have been accommodated there." (*Offices in the Sky*, op. cit., 286–287.)

139 Air conditioning, while in limited use in the thirties, became common only in the late 1940s. Shultz and Simmons stated that "The invention of the fluorescent lamp tripled and quadrupled the use of light in cities and vastly increased the comfort and output potential of workers." (*Offices in the Sky*, op. cit., 202.) In 1960, the Illuminating Engineering Society recommended a standard of 100 footcandles; see Richard S. Wissoker, "More Light for Less," *Buildings* (April 1966): 79.

140 Shultz and Simmons, *Offices in the Sky*, op. cit., 250. With time, glass became the standard material for curtain walls, technology improved, and prices went down. There were experiments with other materials, especially pressed metal panels, but they did not catch on.

141 Fisher, "The Boom in Office Buildings," op. cit.: 32.

142 Quoted in Shultz and Simmons, *Offices in the Sky*, op. cit., 247.

143 Ibid., 248; Yale Robbins, Inc., *Manhattan Office Buildings*, op. cit., 147.

144 Shultz and Simmons, *Offices in the Sky*, op. cit., 248. According to Shultz and Simmons, this type of construction provided two benefits: company departments can be laid out to yield the most efficient work-flow and less space per occupant is required.

145 Ibid., 249. Also see "Office Building Bonanza," *Fortune* (January 1950): 84–86, 127–129.

146 Fisher, "The Boom in Office Buildings," op. cit.: 21. This statistic measures buildings completed from 1947 through the mid-1960s.

147 Ibid.: 21–22, 32.

148 The plan of the Sears Tower is composed of nine parts, each seventy-five feet square. See Saliga, ed., *The Sky's the Limit*, op. cit., 225–226.

149 Planners had calculated that if built out to the maximum under the 1916 zoning, high-rise buildings could house 100 million workers. For a discussion of the aims of the 1961 Resolution, see Roy Strickland, "The 1961 Zoning Revision and the Template of the Ideal City," in Bressi, ed., *Planning and Zoning New York City*, op. cit., 48–60.

150 A building could contain floor area equal to the area of the particular plot, multiplied by a number designated for that zoning district. For example, a building on a 10,000 square-foot lot in a district with an FAR of 10 could contain 100,000 square feet of floor area.
That maximum area could be arranged within any number of floors—in fifteen stories covering the whole site or thirty stories on half of the site, etc. For a discussion of the purposes and particulars of the 1961 zoning resolution, see Norman Marcus, "Zoning from 1961 to 1991: Turning Back the Clock—But with an Up-to-the-Minute Social Agenda," in Bressi, ed., *Planning and Zoning New York City*, op. cit., 61–102, and *Zoning Handbook* (New York: New York City Department of City Planning, 1990), 3–4.

151 Marcus, "Zoning from 1961 to 1991," op. cit.: 63.

152 William Pedersen, "Considerations for Urban Architecture and the Tall Building," in Lynn S. Beedle, ed., *Second Century of the Skyscraper* (New York: Van Nostrand Reinhold, 1988), 162–163.

Part II

1 See Alfred D. Chandler, Jr., *The Visible Hand: The Managerial Revolution in American Business* (Cambridge: Harvard University Press, 1977), and Olivier Zunz, *Making America Corporate* (Chicago: University of Chicago Press, 1990).

2 Thomas Bender and William R. Taylor, "Architecture and Culture: Some Aesthetic Tensions in the Shaping of Modern New York City," in William Sharpe and Leonard Wallock, eds., *Visions of the Modern City* (Baltimore: Johns Hopkins University Press, 1987), 189–219.

3 Zunz, *Making America Corporate*, op. cit., 124.

4 Kenneth Turney Gibbs, *Business Architectural Imagery in America, 1870–1930* (Ann Arbor: University of Michigan Press, 1984), 1.

5 William Jordy, *American Buildings and Their Architects: Progressive Ideals at the Turn of the Twentieth Century* vol.4 (New York: Oxford University Press, 1972), 85.

6 For example, two popular textbooks of the history of architecture, Spiro Kostof, *A History of Architecture: Settings and Rituals,* and Marvin Trachtenberg and Isabelle Hyman, *Architecture from Prehistory to Postmodernism,* discuss only corporate skyscrapers and refer to the clients occupants.

7 Joe R. Feagin and Robert Parker, *Building American Cities: The Urban Real Estate Game* 2nd ed. (Englewood Cliffs, NJ: Prentice Hall, 1990), 104; the chapter cited is titled "Mergers and Mammoth Corporations."

8 Gail Fenske and Deryck Holdsworth, "Corporate Identity and the New York Office Building, 1895–1915," in David Ward and Olivier Zunz, eds., *The Landscape of Modernity* (New York: Russell Sage, 1992), 129.

9 Ibid., 129.

10 Ibid., 135, 143. There were 1,025 tenants in the Woolworth Building in a 1929 city directory. I am indebted to Gail Fenske for photocopies of tenant lists of the Woolworth Building; the one from 1913 came from the Cass Gilbert Collection of the New-York Historical Society; the other, of 1924, came from the Woolworth Company Archives.

11 The mixed-use project combined an office building with upper floors of lodges and meeting rooms for various fraternal orders; see Donald Hoffmann, *The Architecture of John Wellborn Root* (Chicago: University of Chicago Press, 1973), 196–198.

12   A 1929 telephone directory listed 133 tenants in the Bankers Trust Building, of which about half were lawyers or financial services; Fenske and Holdsworth, "Corporate Identity," op. cit., 158, note 49.

13   John Donald Wilson, *The Chase: The Chase Manhattan Bank, N.A., 1945–1985* (Boston: Harvard Business School Press, 1986), 110.

14   Figures supplied by Chase, June 1995.

15   Fenske and Holdsworth, "Corporate Identity," op. cit., 140.

16   Fenske and Holdsworth wrote: "The only justification for the towers was an enterprise's augmented visibility on the urban scene." (154) Other scholars have repeated this point, for example, Olivier Zunz in *Making America Corporate* and William Taylor in *In Pursuit of Gotham.*

17   The first professional organizations for building owners and managers were formed around 1910; data on numbers of tenants and average office size before that time are difficult to find. For floor plans in the early twentieth century, I have relied on early publications by William H. Birkmire, *The Planning and Construction of High Office-Buildings* 2nd ed. (New York: John Wiley & Sons, 1900) and *Skeleton Construction in Buildings* 3rd ed. (New York: John Wiley & Sons, 1900), and Barr Ferree, *The Modern Office Building* (New York: privately printed, 1896).

18   Birkmire, *The Planning and Construction of High Office-Buildings*, op. cit., 70; Ferree, *The Modern Office Building*, op. cit., 51.

19   *New York Standard Guide* (New York: The Foster and Reynolds Company, 1917), 17.

20   In Chicago, offices were slightly larger, usually around 200 to 300 square feet; for example, Sullivan's Schiller Building had offices ranging from 13 x 16 feet to 13 x 19 or 25 feet; see Ferree, *The Modern Office Building*, op. cit., 49. The sixteen- and seventeen-story Manhattan and Old Colony Buildings had about 600 offices; the Monadnock had 1,600; figures are taken from Frank A. Randall, *History of the Development of Building Construction in Chicago* (Urbana: University of Illinois Press, 1949).

21   Figures from Randall, *History of the Development of Building Construction in Chicago*, op. cit., 158, 198.

22   Earle Shultz and Walter Simmons, *Offices in the Sky* (Indianapolis: Bobbs-Merril, 1959), 140. This eighty-eight percent constituted fifty-four percent of all downtown space; the two percent represented fourteen percent of the total. For area per employee, see W. C. Clark and J. L. Kingston, *The Skyscraper: A Study in the Economic Height of Modern Office Buildings* (New York: American Institute of Steel Construction, Inc., 1930), 17.

23   Ibid., 140. The eighty-seven percent represented fifty-two percent of all space; unfortunately, there was no contemporary survey for New York or Chicago.

24   Louis H. Masotti and David C. Davenport, "The Office Report Card," in *Chicago Office*, a publication of the Building Owners and Managers Association of Chicago (1992), 23.

25   An Urban Land Institute survey covering 1946 to 1960 estimated the ratio of speculative to "custom" office buildings in New York to be 3:1; see Robert Moore Fisher, "The Boom in Office Buildings: An Economic Study of the Past Two Decades," *Technical Bulletin* 58 (Washington, DC: Urban Land Institute, 1969): 2, 9. The research of The Real Estate Board of New York found a similar ratio for the years 1947 to 1956: eighty-two percent of the total new space was in competitive buildings; see Gordon D. MacDonald and Real Estate Board of New York Research Department, *Office Building Construction, Manhattan 1947–1967* (New York: Real Estate Board of New York, 1964), 2, 4, 6.

26   As discussed in Part I and below, in the decade after World War II, speculative highrise development in Chicago was greatly reduced. Shultz and Simmons argued that this occurred because the city's height restrictions kept the building smaller than the economic height; thus speculative builders could not make sufficient profits, and so did not build. This conclusion would seem to be supported by the fact that from 1946 to 1960, eighty-five percent of new Chicago buildings were "custom" buildings, including many for government, not-for-profits, and insurance companies. This was precisely the opposite of the custom-to-speculative ratio in New York. See Fisher, "The Boom in Office Buildings," op. cit.: 1–3. Ross Miller discusses the revival of highrise construction in Chicago after 1955 as part of the policy of the new administration of Mayor Daley in his essay, "City Hall and the Architecture of Power: The Rise and Fall of the Dearborn Corridor," in John Zukowsky, ed., *Chicago Architecture and Design, 1923–1993: Reconfiguration of an American Metropolis* (Chicago: The Art Institute of Chicago, and Munich: Prestel, 1993), 246–263.

27   Richard Hurd, *Principles of City Land Values* (New York: The Record and Guide, 1903), 1. Hurd was a self-described "conservative lender on real estate," and was in charge of the Mortgage Department of the U. S. Mortgage and Trust Company.

28   Ibid. Hurd also noted: "The interest on the cost of the building must exceed the average interest rate by an amount equal to the annual depreciation of the building, thus providing a sinking fund sufficient to replace the building at the end of its life." Another clear definition of land value as capitalization of net income was offered by Homer Hoyt: "The income received from a property....Is a joint land and building income, and it is only after the expenses of operating the building are deducted that the residual land income is determined"; Homer Hoyt, *One Hundred Years of Land Values in Chicago* (Chicago: University of Chicago Press, 1933), 449.

29   Hoyt, *One Hundred Years*, op. cit., 449.

30   Ibid. As Hoyt noted, incomes due one hundred years in the future have only a negligible value today, so the value of land was figured for about thirty or forty years. For office buildings, this period represented an average life span, since from the late nineteenth through the early twentieth century, change was so rapid that buildings either became technologically outmoded or were demolished in order to construct a taller, more profitable structure.

31   Ibid., 368–403.

32   Ibid., 369. In brief, Hoyt emphasized the stages of population growth, rent levels and operating costs of existing buildings, new construction, land values, and subdivision activity. He expanded on the idea of the eighteen year cycle in "The Urban Real Estate Cycle: Performances and Prospects," *Technical Bulletin* 38 (Washington, DC: Urban Land Institute, 1960): 1.

33 Roy Wenzlick, *The Coming Boom in Real Estate....And What to Do About It* (New York: Simon and Schuster, 1936), 12.

34 "Skyscrapers: Pyramids in Steel and Stock," *Fortune* 2 (August 1930): 60–61, 73–75.

35 Ibid.: 60.

36 Ibid.: 60–61.

37 The structure that became the Chrysler Building was begun as a speculative venture by William H. Reynolds, who hired the architect William Van Alen to prepare drawings for an office tower he hoped would be the world's tallest. In 1927 Reynolds sold the lease on the plot and the plans to Walter P. Chrysler, who made the building his company's New York headquarters.

38 "Skyscrapers: Pyramids in Steel and Stock," op. cit.: 61. Col. William A. Starrett also described this process in *Skyscrapers and the Men Who Build Them* (New York: Charles Scribner's Sons, 1928), 110.

39 Starrett, *Skyscrapers and the Men Who Build Them*, op. cit., 110.

40 According to Shultz and Simmons, rates could range from five to ten percent, or even up to twenty percent; op. cit., 144. William Starrett gave a slightly different numbers: "The bond houses underwrite the first mortgage bond issues at six to ten points of the principal sum, covering their profit, risk, and distribution costs, and sell the bonds, bearing six percent interest or thereabouts, to the public." Starrett, *Skyscrapers and the Men Who Build Them*, op. cit., 115–117. On the dominance of bond houses in twenties financing, *Fortune* noted that of $20 billion in outstanding mortgages on real estate in 1930, only $4 billion was held by banks; see "Skyscrapers: Pyramids in Steel and Stock," op. cit.: 61.

41 Shultz and Simmons, *Offices in the Sky*, op. cit., 144.

42 Ibid., 144–147.

43 James Grant, *Money of the Mind: Borrowing and Lending in America from the Civil War to Michael Miliken* (New York: Noonday Press, 1992), 161.

44 Shultz and Simmons, *Offices in the Sky*, op. cit., 143 and Grant, *Money of the Mind*, op. cit., 168.

45 James Grant describes how S. W. Straus "slid gradually into questionable practices" in *Money of the Mind*, op. cit., 163–168.

46 Shultz and Simmons, *Offices in the Sky*, op. cit., 145.

47 Ibid., 143.

48 Grant, *Money of the Mind*, op. cit., 170–172.

49 "Warning Signals Raised in Local Construction Field: Continuous Unprecedented Volume of Contracts Awarded in Five Boroughs Causes New York Building Congress to

Advise Caution in Projecting New Operations," *The Record and Guide* 113 (5 April 1924): 7.

50   "Contracts Awarded in 1926 Break All Records for City," *The Record and Guide* 119 (8 January 1927): 9.

51   "Realty Market Conditions Shown by Wide Survey," *The Record and Guide* 123 (5 January 1929): 9; "1928 Greatest Year in Construction Industry," *The Record and Guide* (12 January 1929): 8; Charles F. Noyes, "Noyes Reviews a Successful Real Estate Year," *The Record and Guide* 124 (11 January 1930): 8.

52   Robert H. Armstrong and Homer Hoyt, *Decentralization in New York City* (Chicago: The Urban Land Institute, 1941), 130.

53   Ibid., 147. A survey of vacancy rates in several dozen American cities conducted by a NABOM committee estimated the rate in New York in 1931 to be 17.1 percent; Chicago was 20.3; also see Shultz and Simmons, *Offices in the Sky*, op. cit., 163.

54   Ibid.

55   "Skyscrapers: Pyramids in Steel and Stock," op. cit.: 60.

56   Frederick Lewis Allen, *Only Yesterday: An Informal History of the 1920s* (1931; reprint New York: Harper and Row, 1959), 264.

57   For example, as a result of the spate of twelve- to sixteen-story buildings completed in Chicago in the boom of 1889–1894, all commercial land was revalued as if it contained a sixteen-story building; see Hoyt, *One Hundred Years*, op. cit., 152–153.

58   "Real Estate and Building in 1905," *The Record and Guide* 77 (6 January 1906): 1–3.

59   Marc Weiss has written about the "The Politics of Real Estate Cycles"; see *Business and Economic History* 20 (1991):1–8.

60   Hoyt, *One Hundred Years*, op, cit.; "like tidal waves," 372. Hoyt's remarkable book was the first long-run record of land values for an American city; his data collecting was herculean, and the text is very readable, despite its less-than-gripping title.

61   Ibid., 372.

62   The peaks of the five cycles were 1836, 1853–55, 1869, 1890, and 1925. During the building boom from 1889 to 1892, twenty-one speculative office buildings were erected; see Hoyt, *One Hundred Years*, op. cit., 151. Donald Hoffmann quotes Dankmar Adler as noting that nearly every skyscraper in the city had been erected by a stock company organized for that purpose only; see Hoffman, *The Architecture of John Wellborn Root*, op. cit., 86.

63   Hoyt, *One Hundred Years*, op. cit., 210. Also see the statements to the Chicago Zoning Committee by William Ellis, in which he claimed that the "twelve-story building, the so-called modern fireproof building in Chicago has not been a success," since, except in a few cases where ground rents were particularly low, "the buildings were too good to throw away and not good enough to keep"; *Building Height Limitations* (Chicago: The Chicago Real Estate Board, 1923), 76.

64   The exceptional year when there was little construction was 1908, which reflected the short-lived panic of 1907; Hoyt, *One Hundred Years*, op. cit., 210. The activity in 1910–1911 represented seventeen to twenty percent of the total annual construction, as opposed to three to four percent in other years; Ibid., 224–225, 237.

65   See Hoyt on rising rents, *One Hundred Years*, op. cit., 237–238. Hoyt's fifth cycle spanned the years between 1917 and 1933 (the lows of the curve), with the most vigorous construction during 1923–1929.

66   Depending on the source, rentable space in Chicago in 1920 totaled somewhere between 14 and 17 million square feet; Fisher, "The Boom in Office Buildings," op. cit.: 22, Tables 1 and 14, Chart 3. Other figures in the same study suggest that the total volume of square feet in new office buildings added to the Loop from 1890 to 1919 was approximately 10.5 million.

67   For the explanation of the collapse of bond financing in Chicago, which began in 1928, even before the stock market crash, see Hoyt, *One Hundred Years*, op, cit., 445–446.

68   Office building investment was up by half and represented the highest amount in that category in the city's history; "Real Estate and Building in 1905," *The Record and Guide* 77 (6 January 1906): 1–3.

69   *The Record and Guide* described the real estate market of 1906 as being in a "state of exhaustion." ("A Review and a Prospect," *The Record and Guide* 89 [6 January 1912]: 5.)

70   "Real Estate Review and Prospect," *The Record and Guide* 95 (2 January 1915): 1. Shultz and Simmons noted "a condition of overbuilding and severe rental competition from about 1905–1915." (154)

71   Hurd, *Principles of City Land Values*, op. cit.; map reproduced in Figure 163 appears on page 158.

72   Ibid., Table II, 144.

73   Armstrong and Hoyt, *Decentralization in New York City*, op. cit., 125.

74   The boundaries of Midtown, both north and south and east and west, can be debated; office buildings are most concentrated in the areas noted here. In the 1920s and also today, the real estate industry gives names to several office districts: Grand Central, Plaza, Times Square, and Columbus Circle.

75   Hoyt compiled maps of central Chicago noting land values for eight different years from 1830 to 1931; see *One Hundred Years*, op. cit., 340–341.

76   Ibid., 333. It should be noted, however, that skyscrapers in the 1890s were already spread through various parts of the city.

77   Support also came from owners of existing skyscrapers who wanted to maintain stable rents and protect their property values and from owners of older buildings who objected to the higher valuations for their properties. Hoyt, *One Hundred Years*, op. cit., 153.

The spreading out of the CBD did prevent an extreme rise in land prices; the average Loop increase from 1910 to 1928 was only sixty-two percent; total land value in Loop in 1910 was $600 million; in 1928 it was $1,000 million; Hoyt, *One Hundred Years*, op. cit., 242, 258.

78   Shultz and Simmons, *Offices in the Sky*, op. cit., 283.

79   New York's remarkable dominance in national markets is demonstrated in a group of charts in Armstrong and Hoyt, *Decentralization in New York City*, op. cit., 90–99; for example, it had about forty percent of the country's annual exports and more than half the nation's checks written to individual accounts.

80   "Tall Buildings in American Cities," *The American City* 41 (September 1929): 130.

81   Shultz and Simmons cite 14.3 million square feet of office space in the Loop from 1875 through 1922; *Offices in the Sky*, op. cit., 284.

82   Figures for Chicago, see Fisher, "The Boom in Office Buildings," op. cit.: 22. The figure for New York was 38.6 million; see Gordon D. MacDonald, *Office Building Construction*, op. cit., Table II, 2.

83   In a marketing strategy that recalls the 1890s advice of Owen Aldis, the small floor areas of this yet-to-be-realized speculative tower are targeted at small and medium-sized firms. Descriptions of the height of the tower, designed by architect Cesar Pelli, varies in different accounts; 1914 feet is cited by Paul Goldberger in "In Chicago, a New Romanticism," *The New York Times* (29 October 1989): Sec. 2: 89, and also in Michael Smith, "Buildup: Chicago's Booms with Highrise Construction and Proposals for More," *Inland Architect* 34 (January/February 1990): 48–57.

84   Twice, on two different sites, Donald Trump proposed to erect a record-breaking structure designed by Chicago architect Helmut Jahn; a speculative tower designed by Kohn, Pedersen and Fox (KPF) was proposed for a site at 383 Madison Avenue; all schemes were dropped when met with strong opposition from the public and from the City's planning agency.

85   Lewis Mumford, "Is the Skyscraper Tolerable?" *Architecture* 55 (February 1927): 67–69. His answer was "no."

Illustration Credits

1–6   Collection of the author
7   *Architectural Record* 31 (April 1912): 329.
8   Courtesy of Ryerson and Burnham Libraries, The Art Institute of Chicago
          From G.M. Beattie, *History of the Peoples Gas Building Construction.*
9   *Buildings and Building Management* 25 (8 June 1925): 43.
10   Collection of the Museum of the City of New York
11   *Buildings and Building Management* 25 (31 August 1925): 27.
12   Courtesy of Metropolitan Life Insurance Company
13   Courtesy of Ryerson and Burnham Libraries, The Art Institute of Chicago
          From G.M. Beattie, *History of the Peoples Gas Building Construction.*
14   Collection of the author
15   J. Stübben, *Der Stadtebau* vol. 9, fig. 574.
16   G. W. Bromley, *Atlas of City of Manhattan*, 1889.
17–24   Collection of the author
25   W. H. Birkmire, *The Planning and Construction of High Office-Buildings*,
          2nd ed., 17.
26   W. H. Birkmire, *The Planning and Construction of High Office-Buildings*,
          2nd ed., 75.
27   Collection of the author
28   Avery Architectural and Fine Arts Library, Columbia University
          From rental brochure, real estate brochures collection.
29   Avery Architectural and Fine Arts Library, Columbia University
          From rental brochure, real estate brochures collection.
30   Avery Architectural and Fine Arts Library, Columbia University
          From rental brochure, real estate brochures collection.
31   Courtesy of Galbreath Realty
32   J. Lombardi, *Liberty Tower Report.*
33   *American Architect and Building News* 96 (6 October 1909): 138.

34	Collection of the author
35	Collection of the author
36	*Buildings and Building Management* 15 (May 1915): 24.
37	Collection of the author
38	Collection of the author
39	Chicago Historical Society
40	F. Randall, *History of the Development of Building Construction in Chicago*, 153.
41	Collection of the author
42	Collection of the author
43	Collection of Penny Kleinman
44	Collection of Penny Kleinman
45	Collection of the author
46	F. Randall, *History of the Development of Building Construction in Chicago*, 179.
47	*Prominent Buildings Erected by the George A. Fuller Company*, 30.
48	*Prominent Buildings Erected by the George A. Fuller Company*, 30.
49	Collection of Penny Kleinman
50	*Scribners Magazine* 15 (March 1894): 318.
51	*Engineering Record* 27 (January 1893): 160.
52	Collection of Penny Kleinman
53	Collection of Penny Kleinman
54–61	Collection of the author
62	From *Prominent Buildings Erected by the George A. Fuller Company* (1893), np.
63	*Architectural Record* 38 (July 1915): 118.
64	*Architectural Record* 38 (July 1915): 65.
65	*Architectural Record* 38 (July 1915): 102.
66	Collection of Penny Kleinman
67	*Prominent Buildings Erected by the George A. Fuller Company*, 42.
68	Collection of the author
69	*Architectural Record* 31 (February 1912): 321.
70	Collection of the author
71	Courtesy of Ryerson and Burnham Libraries, The Art Institute of Chicago
72–77	Collection of the author
78	*Architectural Forum* 52 (June 1930): 882.
79–87	Collection of the author
88	*American Architect and Building News* 138 (October 1930): 31.
89	*Architecural Forum* (September 1930): 800.
90	*Buildings and Building Management* (16 June 1930): 53.
91–93	Collection of the author
94	*Real Estate Record and Builders' Guide* (December 1928): 7.
95	Courtesy Hagley Mueum and Library, Wilmington, Delaware From Longwood Manuscripts 229-15, Box lot 5, file 26, I.
96	Collection of the author From *Architectural Record* 67 (1930): 339.
97	Collection of the author From *Architectural Forum* 53 (July 1930): 98.
98	Empire State Building Archives, Avery Architectural and Fine Arts Library, Columbia University
99–103	Collection of the author
104	Chicago Historical Society
105	Collection of the author

106	Courtesy of Ryerson and Burnham Libraries, The Art Institute of Chicago
107	*Architectural Record* 67 (June 1930): 187.
108	Collection of the author
109	Graham, *The Architecture of Graham, Anderson, Probst and White* (1933).
110	Collection of the author
111	Graham, *The Architecture of Graham, Anderson, Probst and White* (1933).
112–118	Collection of the author
119	*Architectural Record* (July 1930): 16.
120–122	Collection of the author
123	Courtesy of Ryerson and Burnham Libraries, The Art Institute of Chicago
124–126	Collection of the author
127	Collection of the author
	Plans from *Buildings and Building Management* (25 August 1930): 60.
128	Collection of the author
129	Courtesy of Ryerson and Burnham Libraries, The Art Institute of Chicago
	From rental brochure.
130	Collection of the author
131	Collection of the author
132	Collection of the Museum of the City of New York
133	*Buildings and Building Management* 25 (16 February 1925): 39.
134	From J. Pile, *Interiors Third Book of Offices.*
135–138	Collection of the author
139	Hugh Ferriss Collection, Drawings and Archives, Avery Architectural and Fine Arts Library, Columbia University
140–142	Collection of the author
143	Photograph by the author
144	Photograph by the author
145–147	Collection of the author
148	Courtesy of New-York Historical Society
149–153	Collection of the author
154	Courtesy of Alfred Mainzer, Inc., Long Island City, NY 11101
155	Collection of the author
156	*Technical Bulletin* 38 (1960): 7.
157	*Real Estate Record and Builders Guide* 95 (2 January 1915): 4.
158	*Fortune* 2 (August 1930): 6.
159	R. Armstrong and H. Hoyt, *Decentralization in New York City*, 147.
160–161	Collection of the author
162	Shultz and Simmons, *Offices in the Sky.*
163	Hurd, *Principles of City Land Values*, 158.
164	Collection of the author
165	Hoyt, *One Hundred Years.*
166–168	Collection of the author
169	Collection of the Museum of the City of New York
170	Collection of Penny Kleinman

Select Bibliography

Journals consulted:
American Architect and Building News
Architectural Forum
Architectural Record
Buildings and Building Management
Inland Architect
Journal of the Society of Architectural Historians
Real Estate Record and Builders Guide

Architectural Forum, special issue on office buildings (September 1930).

Architectural Record 38, special issue on "Daniel H. Burnham and His Associates" (July 1915).

Armstrong, Robert and Homer Hoyt. *Decentralization in New York*. Chicago: Urban Land Institute, 1941.

Atlas of the City of New York, Borough of Manhattan. Philadelphia: G. W. Bromley and Company, 1899.

Beedle, Lynn S., ed. *Second Century of the Skyscraper*. New York: Van Nostrand Reinhold, 1988.

Berger, Miles. *They Built Chicago: Entrepreneurs Who Shaped a Great City's Architecture*. Chicago: Bonus Books, 1992.

Birkmire, William H. *The Planning and Construction of High Office-Buildings*, 2nd ed. New York: John Wiley & Sons, 1900.

———. *Skeleton Construction in Buildings*, 3rd ed. New York: John Wiley & Sons, 1900.

Bletter, Rosemarie Haag. "The Invention of the Skyscraper: Notes on its Diverse Histories," *Assemblage* no. 2 (February 1987).

Bluestone, Daniel. *Constructing Chicago*. New Haven: Yale University Press, 1991.

Bragdon, Claude. "Architecture in the United States: The Skyscraper," *Architectural Record* 26 (August 1909): 84–96.

Bressi, Todd W., ed. *Planning and Zoning New York City, Yesterday, Today, and Tomorrow*. New Brunswick: Center for Urban Policy Research, Rutgers University, 1993.

Breugmann, Robert, ed. *Holabird and Roche and Holabird and Root: An Illustrated Catalog of Works, 1880–1940*, 3 vols. New York: Garland, 1991.

———. "The Marquette Building and the Myth of the Chicago School," *Threshold* (Fall 1991).

Chappell, Sally A. Kitt. *Architecture and Planning of Graham, Anderson, Probst and White, 1912–1936*. Chicago: University of Chicago Press, 1992.

Chase, W. Parker. *New York: The Wonder City*. New York: Wonder City Publishing, 1932.

Clark, W. C. and J. L. Kingston. *The Skyscraper: A Study in the Economic Height of Modern Office Buildings*. New York: American Institute of Steel Construction, Inc., 1930.

Condit, Carl. *Chicago, 1910–1929*. Chicago: University of Chicago Press, 1973

——. *The Chicago School of Architecture*. Chicago: University of Chicago Press, 1964.

——. *The Rise of the Skyscraper*. Chicago: University of Chicago Press, 1952

Corbett, Harvey Wiley. "New Stones for Old," three-part series, *Saturday Evening Post* 198 (27 March, 8 May, 15 May 1926).

Cronon, William. *Nature's Metropolis: Chicago and the Great West*. New York: Norton, 1991.

Domosh, Mona. *Scrapers of the Sky: The Symbolic and Functional Structures of Lower Manhattan*. Ph.D., Department of Geography, Clark University, MA, 1985.

Evers, Cecil C. *The Commercial Problem in Buildings*. New York: The Real Estate Record and Builders Guide, 1914.

Fenske, Gail and Deryck Holdsworth. "Corporate Identity and the Modern Office Building, 1895–1915," in David Ward and Olivier Zunz, eds., *The Landscape of Modernity*. New York: Russell Sage, 1992.

Ferree, Barr. "Economic Conditions of Architecture in America," *Proceedings of the Twenty-Seventh Annual Convention of the American Institute of Architects* (Chicago: Inland Architect, 1893).

——. "The High Building in Art," *Scribners Magazine* (March 1884).

——. *The Modern Office Building*. New York: privately printed, 1896.

Fisher, Robert Moore. "The Boom in Office Buildings: An Economic Study of the Past Two Decades," *Technical Bulletin* 58 (Washington, DC: Urban Land Institute, 1969).

Fleming, Robins. "For and Against the Skyscraper," *Civil Engineering* (June 1935).

——. "A Half Century of the Skyscraper," *Civil Engineering* (December 1934).

——. "Whence the Skyscraper?" *Civil Engineering* (October 1934).

Ford, George B. *New York City Building Zone Resolution*. New York: New York Title and Mortgage Company, 1920.

Fortune, skyscraper series, vol. 2, nos. 1–6 (July–December, 1930).

Gad, Gunter and Deryck Holdsworth. "Corporate Capitalism and the Emergence of the High-Rise Office Building," *Urban Geography* 8, vol. 3 (1987).

Gibbs, Kenneth Turney. *Business Architectural Imagery in America, 1870–1930*. Ann Arbor: University of Michigan Research Press, 1984.

Goldberger, Paul. *The Skyscraper*. New York: Knopf, 1981.

Graham, Ernest R. *The Architectural Work of Graham, Anderson, Probst and White*. London: Batsford, 1933.

Harrison, Wallace K. "Office Buildings," in Talbot Hamlin, ed., *Forms and Functions of Twentieth Century Architecture*. New York: Columbia University Press, 1952.

Hill, George. "The Economy of the Office Building," *Architectural Record* (1904).

——. "Some Practical Conditions in the Design of the Modern Office Building," *Architectural Record* 2 (1893).

——. "Wasted Opportunities, No. III," *Architectural Record* 3 (1893).

Hines, Thomas F. *Burnham of Chicago, Architect and Planner*. Chicago: University of Chicago Press, 1979.

Hoffmann, Donald. *The Architecture of John Wellborn Root*. Chicago: University of Chicago Press, 1973.

Horowitz, Louis and Boyden Sparkes. *The Towers of New York: The Memoirs of a Master Builder*. New York: Simon and Schuster, 1937.

Hoyt, Homer. *One Hundred Years of Land Values in Chicago*. Chicago: University of Chicago Press, 1933.

——. "The Urban Real Estate Cycle: Performances and Prospects," *Technical Bulletin* 38 (Washington, DC: Urban Land Institute, 1960).

Hurd, Richard M. *Principles of City Land Values*. New York: The Real Estate Record and Builders Guide, 1903.

Huxtable, Ada Louise. *The Tall Building Artistically Reconsidered*. New York: Pantheon, 1984.

Irish, Sharon. "A Machine That Makes the Land Pay: The West Street Building in New York," *Technology and Culture* 30 (April 1989).

Jacobs, Jane. *The Death and Life of Great American Cities*. New York: Vintage, 1961.

Jordy, William H. "The Tall Buildings," in Wim de Wit, ed., *Louis Sullivan: The Function of Ornament*. New York: Norton, 1986.

Kilham, Walter H., Jr. *Raymond Hood, Architect*. New York: Architectural Book Publishing Co., 1973.

Koolhaas, Rem. *Delirious New York*. New York: Oxford University Press, 1978.

Krinsky, Carol Hershelle. *Rockefeller Center*. New York: Oxford University Press, 1978.

——. "Sister Cities," in John Zukowsky, ed., *Chicago and New York: Architectural Interactions*. Chicago: The Art Institute of Chicago, 1984.

Lamb, William F. "The Empire State Building: The General Design," *Architectural Forum* 53 (January 1930).

Landau, Sarah Bradford. "The Tall Office Building Artistically Reconsidered: Arcaded Buildings of the New York School c.1870–1890," in Helen Searing, ed., *In Search of Modern Architecture*. New York: Architectural History Foundation, and Cambridge: MIT Press, 1982.

Lipson, Enoch. *The Effects of Technological Innovation on the Design of Office Buildings in New York City from the Bayard-Condict Building to the Seagram Building*. MA Architectural Technology, Columbia University Graduate School of Planning and Preservation, NY, 1970.

MacDonald, Gordon D. and Real Estate Board of New York Research Department. *Office Building Construction, Manhattan 1901–1953*. New York: Real Estate Board of New York, 1952.

——. *Office Building Construction, Manhattan 1947–1967*. New York: Real Estate Board of New York, 1964.

Mayer, Harold M. and Richard C. Wade. *Chicago: Growth of a Metropolis*. Chicago: University of Chicago Press, 1969.

Mujica, Francisco. *History of the Skyscraper*. New York: Architectural Press, 1930.

Nichols, Charles M., ed. *Studies on Building Height Limitations in Large Cities with Special Reference to Conditions in Chicago, Proceedings of an Investigation of Building Height Limitations Conducted Under the Auspices of the Zoning Committee of the Chicago Real Estate Board, Zoning Committee of the Chicago Real Estate Board in 1923*. Chicago: The Chicago Real Estate Board, 1923.

"Office Building Bonanza," *Fortune* (January 1950).

Pelli, Cesar. "Skyscrapers," *Perspecta* (1982).

Pile, John, ed. *Interiors Second Book of Offices*. New York: Whitney Library of Design, 1969.

——. *Interiors Third Book of Offices*. New York: Whitney Library of Design, 1976.

Rachlis, Eugene and John E. Marquee. *The Land Lords*. New York: Random House, 1963.

Randall, Frank A. *History of the Development of Building Construction in Chicago*. Urbana: University of Illinois Press, 1949.

"Record of Testimony and Statements in Relation to the Necessity for Districting Plan," in *The Final Report of the Commission on Building Districts and Restrictions*. New York: Board of Estimate and Apportionment, 1916.

Report of the Heights of Buildings Commission. New York: Board of Estimate and Apportionment, 1913.

Revell, Keith. "Regulating the Landscape: Real Estate Values, City Planning, and the 1916 Zoning Ordinance," in David Ward and Olivier Zunz, eds., *The Landscape of Modernity*. New York: Russell Sage, 1992.

Robinson, Cervin and Rosemarie Haag Bletter. *Skyscraper Style: Art Deco New York*. New York: Oxford University Press, 1975.

Rosenauer, Michael. *Modern Office Buildings*. London: Batsford, 1955.

Roth, Leland. *A Concise History of American Architecture*. New York: Harper and Row, 1980.

Saliga, Pauline A., ed. *The Sky's the Limit: A Century of Chicago Skyscrapers*. New York: Rizzoli, 1990.

Sexton, R.W. *American Commercial Buildings of Today*. New York: Architectural Book Publishing, 1928.

Shultz, Earle and Walter Simmons. *Offices in the Sky*. Indianapolis: Bobbs-Merrill, 1959.

Staemper, John W. *Chicago's North Michigan Avenue: Planning and Development, 1900–1930*. Chicago: University of Chicago Press, 1991.

Starrett, Paul. *Changing the Skyline*. New York: Whittlesey House, 1938.

Starrett, Col. William. *Skyscrapers and the Men Who Build Them*. New York: Charles Scribner's Sons, 1928.

Stern, Robert A.M., Gregory Gilmartin, and John Montague Massengale. *New York 1900*. New York: Rizzoli, 1983.

——, Gregory Gilmartin, and Thomas Mellins. *New York 1930*. New York: Rizzoli, 1987.

——, Thomas Mellins, and David Fishman. *New York 1960*. New York: The Monacelli Press, 1995.

Sullivan, Louis H. "The Tall Building Artistically Considered," in *Kindergarten Chats and Other Writings*. New York: Dover, 1918; repr., 1979.

Susman, Warren. *Culture as History*. New York: Pantheon, 1984.

Taylor, William R. *In Pursuit of Gotham: Culture and Commerce in New York*. New York: Oxford University Press, 1992.

Toll, Seymour L. *Zoned American*. New York: Grossman, 1969.

Urban Land Institute. *Tall Office Buildings in the United States*. Washington: Urban Land Institute, 1984.

Van Leeuwen, Thomas A.P. *The Skyward Trend of Thought*. The Hague: AHA Books, 1986.

Ward, David and Olivier Zunz, eds. *The Landscape of Modernity*. New York: Russell Sage, 1992.

Weisman, Winston. "A New View of Skyscraper History," in Edgar Kaufmann, Jr., *The Rise of an American Architecture*. New York: Praeger and the Metropolitan Museum of Art, 1970.

Weiss, Marc. "Density and Intervention: New York's Planning Traditions," in David Ward and Olivier Zunz, eds., *The Landscape of Modernity*. New York: Russell Sage, 1992.

——. "The Politics of Real Estate Cycles," *Business and Economic History* 20 (1991).

Willis, Carol. "A 3-D CBD: How the 1916 Zoning Law Shaped Manhattan's Central Business Districts," in Todd W. Bressi, ed., *Planning and Zoning New York City, Yesterday, Today, and Tomorrow*. New Brunswick: Center for Urban Policy Research, Rutgers University, 1993.

——. "Form Follows Finance: The Empire State Building and the Forces that Shaped It," in David Ward and Olivier

Zunz, eds., *The Landscape of Modernity*. New York: Russell Sage, 1992.

——. "Light, Height, and Site: The Skyscraper in Chicago," in John Zukowsky, ed., *Chicago Architecture and Design, 1923–1993: Reconfiguration of an American Metropolis*. Chicago: The Art Institute of Chicago, and Munich: Prestel, 1993.

——. "Zoning and Zeitgeist: The Skyscraper City in the 1920s," *Journal of the Society of Architectural Historians* (March 1986).

Winkler, Franz. "Some Chicago Buildings Represented by the Work of Holabird and Root," *Architectural Record* 31 (April 1912).

Yale Robbins, Inc. *Manhattan Office Buildings*. New York: Yale Robbins, Inc., 1983.

Zoning Handbook. New York: New York City Department of City Planning, 1990.

Zukowsky, John, ed. *Chicago Architecture, 1872–1922: Birth of a Metropolis* Chicago: The Art Institute of Chicago, and Munich: Prestel, 1987.

——. *Chicago Architecture and Design, 1923–1993: Reconfiguration of an American Metropolis*. Chicago: The Art Institute of Chicago, and Munich: Prestel, 1993.

——. *Chicago and New York: Architectural Interactions*. Chicago: The Art Institute of Chicago, 1984.

Zunz, Olivier. *Making America Corporate, 1870–1920*. Chicago: University of Chicago Press, 1990.

Index

About the Author

Carol Willis is an architectural historian who teaches in the
"Shape of Two Cities: New York and Paris" program at Columbia
University's School of Architecture, Planning, and Preservation.
She is an adjunct assistant professor of Urban Studies at
Columbia College, and the author of numerous articles on architecture and
urbanism. As curator of an exhibition of the drawings of Hugh Ferriss,
she edited the reprint of Ferriss's 1929 book,
The Metropolis of Tomorrow (Princeton Architectural Press, 1986).
Ms. Willis lives in a skyscraper in the middle of Manhattan.